We Knew Him

We Knew Him

Personal Encounters with Jesus of Nazareth

George H. Dawe

Foreword by
Roy D. King
Former General Superintendent
Pentecostal Assemblies of Newfoundland and Labrador

Edited by
Burton K. Janes
Editor, *Beyond Aslan: Essays on C.S. Lewis*

WestBow
PRESS
A DIVISION OF THOMAS NELSON

Scripture taken from the Holy Bible, NEW INTERNATIONAL VERSION®. Copyright © 1973, 1978, 1984 by Biblica, Inc. All rights reserved worldwide. Used by permission. NEW INTERNATIONAL VERSION® and NIV® are registered trademarks of Biblica, Inc. Use of either trademark for the offering of goods or services requires the prior written consent of Biblica US, Inc.

WestBow Press books may be ordered through booksellers or by contacting:

WestBow Press
A Division of Thomas Nelson
1663 Liberty Drive
Bloomington, IN 47403
www.westbowpress.com
1-(866) 928-1240

ISBN: 978-1-4497-4912-5 (sc)

Library of Congress Control Number: 2012907595

Printed in the United States of America

WestBow Press rev. date: 05/03/2012

*This book is
affectionately dedicated
in memory of
my father, Clarence Dawe (1917-88),
and my mother, Mary Jane Dawe (1918-2002),
who instilled in me
a love for God and man,
a respect for God's Word,
and an appreciation for family and friends.*

Table of Contents

Foreword. ix

Introduction xiii

  1. Mary. 1

  2. Caiaphas. 9

  3. Pilate 17

  4. Herod. 25

  5. Nicodemus 31

  6. John the Beloved. 37

  7. Peter 41

  8. John Mark 49

  9. John the Baptist 57

10. Judas Iscariot 63

11. Barabbas. 69

12. Simon of Cyrene. 77

13. The Nail-and-Hammer Man. 87

14. Thomas. 95

15. The Penitent Thief 101

16. Lazarus 107

17. Cleopas and Mary. 113

18. Paul 119

Appendix. 125

Works Cited 137

Acknowledgements 145

Foreword

"Then I said, 'Here I am, I have come—it is written about me in the scroll. I desire to do your will, O my God; your law is within my heart'" (Psalm 40:7-8).

"Therefore, when Christ came into the world, he said: 'Sacrifice and offering you did not desire, but a body you prepared for me'" (Hebrews 10:5).

I t is clear that Jesus identified Himself as the exclusive character of Scripture–"it is written about me in the scroll."

George H. Dawe has taken a number of biblical characters, in the first person singular, and allowed them to bear witness to the unique person of Jesus. You will read the clarity of their witness as they affirm the words and works of the Son of Righteousness.

Mary humbly and proudly attests that she is the mother. You will live with her, from the exultation of His birth to her sorrow at the Cross. You will weigh heavily her closing statement of loss and gain at the Cross, "I had lost a Son, but gained a Savior!" George puts to rest the false allusion of her Immaculate Conception and bodily resurrection.

Caiaphas, who condemned Jesus to die, confesses that, through greed, blindness and prejudice, he had become an apostate High Priest. He contrasts the glory that God meant for His priesthood as torn garments, rags for the ash heap.

Pilate could not find any fault worthy of death in Jesus. He confesses that he yielded to mob pressure and political prestige, ignored the jurisprudence of Roman Law, and sentenced Him to crucifixion. The author leaves all who ignore Jesus with Pilate's haunting question, "What shall I do, then, with Jesus who is called Christ?" (Matthew 27:22).

The author continues his chronology of confessors of Jesus, the Son of God, with the host of the Passover Supper. John Mark, the owner of the house, gives the delicate detail that went into the preparations for the last meal Jesus enjoyed with His disciples before His arrest, trial and crucifixion. It was an honor for Jesus to direct that the meal was to be served at *his* house. To be privy to Jesus and His disciples' conversation engraved love, loyalty and gratitude on his heart, leading to his personal martyrdom.

Barabbas testifies to his guilt as bandit and robber and his amazement that he was released from crucifixion in favor of the innocent Jesus. Jesus becomes his substitute, dying in his place. He said that if he had known fully what was happening, he would have used a line from Shakespeare regarding Brutus:

> *His life was gentle, and the elements*
> *So mix'd in him,*
> *That Nature might stand up*
> *And say to all the world, "This was a man!"*

An unnamed soldier identifies himself as the man with the hammer. He tells of his callous heart and the pleasure he and his fellow soldiers received in carrying out Roman law for guilty criminals.

But, this crucifixion was different because of the Man on the center cross.

He was mocked and scorned, receiving treatment beyond humiliation. Inexplicable events were happening, and one of the centurions cried out, "Surely he was the Son of God" (Matthew 27:54).

There is a testimony of hope from the penitent thief. Jesus assured him he would be with Him in Paradise that very day. His troubled conscience became free, knowing that he, a common robber, was going to be with Him. The thief thought he had known Him for ever, for he called Him Jesus.

Lazarus, who had been dead four days, spoke freely and convincingly of his personal death and resurrection. His experience was for God's glory. And, he was assured of a second resurrection.

Perhaps the most convincing witnesses were Cleopas and Mary. They testified that an unknown stranger had joined them while journeying home. He had expounded to them what Moses and the Prophets had written concerning the mysterious happenings in Jerusalem. But, while breaking bread together, He revealed His identity to them. It was Jesus. They hurried back to Jerusalem and told the disciples and others that He was alive.

George shares with his readers the likelihood of the emotions, relevance and heartbeat of those who witnessed Jesus–God "appeared in a body, was vindicated by the Spirit" (1 Timothy 3:16).

Roy D. King
Grand Falls–Windsor, NL

Introduction

Let me introduce you to people who made eternal decisions regarding Jesus of Nazareth. In their past, they had personal encounters with Jesus, resulting in some of them believing on Him and serving Him to their death.

This is a series of eighteen monologues constructed from personal accounts described in the four Gospels, where popular individuals "return" to tell their stories. Actually, I slip into their sandals and give details involving such people as Mary, Herod, Nicodemus, Peter, Judas, Barabbas, Lazarus and Paul.

I invite you to journey with me from eternity to the land of Israel. Let your imagination bring the past into the present, as I describe incidents in Jesus' life, which ends on His cross and climaxes at His empty tomb.

You will also read excerpts from other authors, who combine their knowledge to bring glory to God. This book is intended as a testimony to all who can say, *We Knew Him*.

—*George H. Dawe*

1
Mary

"Near the cross of Jesus stood his mother"
(John 19:25)

I knew Jesus because I was His mother, Mary. That alone would put my name in any Mothers' Hall of Fame. But, what's unique is that I became a mother without knowing a man!

As a woman of hope, I belonged to that group which waited "for the consolation of Israel" (Luke 2:25). I looked for the One "desired of all nations" (Haggai 2:7). However, little did I know that I would be that One's mother.

When God sent the angel Gabriel to announce my pregnancy, he said I was "highly favored" (Luke 1:28). That is, God "bestowed" His grace on me. So, I was a receiver, not a dispenser, of divine grace.

At that time, I was a virgin; a young, unmarried girl. In fact, I was so bewildered I asked Gabriel, "How will this be...since I am a virgin?" (Luke 1:34). I believed Gabriel, but I did not understand how it could be accomplished.

Explaining it years later, John MacArthur writes, "Mary understood that the angel was speaking of an immediate conception, and she and Joseph were still in the midst of the long betrothal or engagement period..., before the actual marriage and consummation." So, Joseph and I did not have sexual relations until after Jesus was born (Matthew 1:25).

The angel's answer put me somewhat at ease. He explained, "The Holy Spirit will come upon you, and the power of the Most High will overshadow you. So the holy one to be born will be called the Son of God" (Luke 1:35). I then accepted the angel's message because, intuitively, I believed that, in the words of one of your scholars, Friedrich August Tholuck, "God never exalts any one who does not humble himself."

Gabriel encouraged me further by saying that my cousin Elizabeth "is going to have a child in her old age, and she who was said to be barren is in her sixth month. For nothing is impossible with God." And, I confirmed my acceptance by declaring, "I am the Lord's servant.... May it be to me as you have said" (Luke 1:36-38). Then, Gabriel disappeared.

I could hardly wait to visit Elizabeth. She was so excited to see me that her baby boy leaped in her womb and she was filled with the Holy Spirit. She suddenly exclaimed, "Blessed are you among women, and blessed is the child you will bear! But why am I so favored, that the mother of my Lord should come to me?" (Luke 1:42-43). When I heard that, I felt my fetus jump for joy. And, Elizabeth responded, "Blessed is she who has believed that what the Lord has said to her will be accomplished!" (Luke 1:45).

At that point, I burst into my "Magnificat," singing, "My soul glorifies the Lord and my spirit rejoices in God my Savior..." (Luke 1:46-47). I was pleased God had chosen me.

Early Church leaders would say that my hymn was the first Christian hymn. And, Augustine, one of the Church Fathers, remarks that such a hymn was "praise to God with a song." One of your Bible scholars, Ray Summers, explains that Mary's song was "her emotional response to God's mighty work in her life and in the life of the people of Israel.... The total of Mary's 'inner being' expressed itself in praise."

I stayed with Elizabeth for about three months, before returning home to Nazareth. I would never forget my visit with her. In fact, my song kept reverberating in my soul. For, in it, I recognized God as my Savior and I personally expressed my need of Him. I knew I was not free from original sin, nor was I immaculate. I too needed God's grace.

Around that time, Elizabeth's son, John, was born. When everyone asked, "What then is this child going to be?," his father, Zechariah, prophesied, "you, my child, will be called a prophet of the Most High; for you will go on before the Lord to prepare the way for him, to give his people the knowledge of salvation through the forgiveness of their sins" (Luke 1:66, 76-77).

In the words of Fulton J. Sheen, when I was due to "give God a human nature," I was more than ready. Because I had been impregnated by the Holy Spirit, I was not ashamed to ratify my pledge to marry Joseph. Meanwhile, we traveled to Bethlehem to have our citizenship registered. And, as Luke records, "While they were there, the time came for the baby to be born, and she gave birth to her firstborn, a son. She wrapped him in cloths and placed him in a manger, because there was no room for them in the inn" (Luke 2:6-7).

For the next few days, life was quite hectic, yet exciting. Angels announced "good news of great joy" (Luke 2:10), shepherds were terrified by "the glory of the Lord" (Luke 2:9), and Wise Men brought gifts from the East. Joseph and I were in the middle of it all.

Everyone seemed happy...everyone, that is, except King Herod. In fact, he ordered the slaughter of all male infants under two. For Joseph and me to escape this travesty, an angel directed him to take us to Egypt until Herod's death. After he died, the angel advised us to return to Israel, where we settled in Nazareth, in northern Galilee.

When Jesus was eight days old, it was time to circumcise him, give him his name, and present him to the Lord (Exodus 13:2, 12). To do this, we offered "a pair of doves" as our sacrifice (Luke 2:24).

Simeon, a righteous man, had been told "by the Holy Spirit that he would not die before he had seen the Lord's Christ" (Luke 2:26). So, still influenced by the Spirit, he went into the Temple courts, took my baby into his arms and sang: "Sovereign Lord, as you have promised, you now dismiss your servant in peace. For my eyes have seen your salvation, which you have prepared in the sight of all people, a light for revelation to the Gentiles and for glory to your people Israel" (Luke 2:29-32).

Joseph and I were amazed. But Simeon was not finished. He turned to me and prophesied, "This child is destined to cause the falling and rising of many in Israel, and to be a sign that will be spoken against, so that the thoughts of many hearts will be revealed. And a sword will pierce your own soul too" (Luke 2:34-35).

What did all that mean? Actually, Simeon was predicting my sorrow. He was saying God's plough would make emotional and spiritual furrows on my heart and brow. Sheen writes: "Other mothers become conscious of motherhood through physical changes within them; [I] became conscious through a spiritual change wrought by the Holy Spirit."

When Jesus was twelve, Joseph and I took him to the one-day Passover Feast in Jerusalem. The Feast of Unleavened Bread immediately followed for one week.

On the way home, we "lost" Jesus. We thought He was somewhere in the caravan. However, after three days, we found Him in the Temple, listening to the scribes and asking them questions (Luke 2:41-46). The teachers were amazed at His answers. But, in an obviously worried tone, I asked Him, "Son, why have you treated us like this? Your father and I have been anxiously searching for you" (Luke 2:48).

My Son replied, "Why were you searching for me?.... Didn't you know I had to be in my Father's house?" (Luke 2:49). Neither Joseph nor I understood what He meant. But, home in Nazareth, I "treasured all these things in [my] heart" (Luke 2:51).

In your New Testament, Mark identifies Jesus as my Son (Mark 6:3). Usually, it was Jewish practice to identify sons by their fathers' name. However, when fathers were unknown, sons were known by their mothers' name. In Jesus' case, Joseph was not His biological father, but His legal father.

When Jesus referred to "my Father's house," Joseph and I were confused. We appreciated that He wanted a relationship with God and were pleased to see His obvious devotion to the Temple. But, we wondered, "Is there more to it? Will we lose our control of Him?" However, we were happy to learn that He would be subject to us. David Gooding explains: "The learned doctors knew their Old Testament inside out. In all the long biblical record, not even Moses who had built the tabernacle, not David who had longed to build the temple, not Solomon who had actually built it, no king or commoner, not the most exalted of them, had ever referred to the tabernacle or temple as 'my Father's house.' "

As Jesus' mother, I was interested in and proud of all His accomplishments. I attended His first miracle at a wedding in Cana of Galilee. When they ran out of wine, I informed Jesus, "They have no more wine." Jesus responded, "Dear woman, why do you involve me?.... My time has not yet come." With that, I instructed the servants, "Do whatever he tells you" (John 2:3-5).

Really, I was asking for a miracle, which would be a sign of Jesus' deity and the beginning of His death. At that moment, I would not be called "mother," but "woman."

What was Jesus saying to me? In Sheen's words, simply this: "My dear mother, do you realize that you are asking Me to proclaim My Divinity–to appear before the world as the Son of God, and to prove my Divinity by My works and My miracles? The moment that I do this, I begin the royal road to the Cross. When I am no longer known among men as the son of the carpenter, but as the Son of God, that will be My first step toward Calvary. My Hour is not yet come; but would you have Me anticipate it? Is it your will that I go to the Cross? If I do, your relationship to Me changes. You are now my mother. You are known everywhere in our little village as the mother of Jesus. But if I appear now as the Savior of men, and begin the work of Redemption, your role will change too."

When my Son used the word "hour," He was referring to His cross. He was saying, again in Sheen's words, that "the time appointed for beginning the task of Redemption was not yet at hand."

Ever since the angel mentioned the word "sword," I knew that my Son did not become man so He could eat, work and sleep like a man. Nor did He become man to fearlessly still the raging tempests. No, He became man to identify with man and die for mans' sin. That's the Incarnation, "the mystery of godliness" (1 Timothy 3:16).

Eventually, I became known as the "Virgin of Sorrows." In fact, while other sons were born to live, my Son was born to die. As prophesied, He was "the Lamb that was slain from the creation of the world" (Revelation

13:8). As Erwin W. Lutzer explains, "If she was to have a son, she was also to have a sword."

The day of Jesus' death was extremely hard for me. I felt all alone. But, while I watched and waited at His cross, He saw me and provided for my loneliness. However, the sword which pierced my heart the most was the soldiers gambling. They were "casting lots," or drawing names, for Jesus' seamless tunic, his undergarment (John 19:23-24). Charles R. Swindoll explains it this way: "His outer garments were insignificant.... But when they touched the tunic, they touched something very near to His heart–the garment made for Him by His mother." Then, John tells us, "Near the cross of Jesus stood his mother" (John 19:25).

For me, the sword was piercing my heart too soon. I still was not finished rejoicing over His birth and ministry. But, as Arthur W. Pink points out, "Never such bliss at a human birth, never such sorrow at an inhuman death."

In my final moments at Calvary, I stood beneath His cross, staring up at His countenance. I saw His marred face and thorn-pierced brow. They say there was thunder, lightening and darkness, but I was oblivious to it all. I saw His blood and felt His pain. I heard the robber and soldiers accuse Him. And, I heard my Son say, "Father, forgive them, for they do not know what they are doing" (Luke 23:34).

In response to the repentant robber, Jesus assured him, "I tell you the truth, today you will be with me in paradise" (Luke 23:43).

Then, to express His own aloneness and identify Himself as David's suffering one, He exclaimed, "My God, my God, why have you forsaken me?" (Matthew 27:46; Psalm 22:1).

Around that time, Jesus paid special attention to John, the beloved disciple, and me, saying, "Dear woman, here is your son," and to John, "Here is your mother" (John 19:26-27). At that moment, John took me to his home.

One of your authors, John Alexander McElroy, tells the following story.

"There is a well-known painting of Mary, brokenhearted. John is leading her away from the crucifixion. On Mary's face the artist has pictured her sorrow. But in her hand she is carrying (would you have dared paint it this way?) the crown of thorns. In the artist's imagining, Mary had 'stood by' until the very end. And when they took Jesus down from the cross she had taken the crown of thorns from His lifeless head. Only then, with the crown of thorns in her hand, was Mary willing to leave the cross."

Jesus made three more statements from the Cross. Knowing that Scripture would be fulfilled, He said, "I am thirsty." Someone soaked a sponge in wine vinegar, putting "the sponge on a stalk of the hyssop plant, and lifted it to Jesus' lips. When he had received the drink, Jesus said, 'It is finished' " (John 19:28-30). Then, as He bowed His head, darkness covered the hill for three hours, and the curtain of the Temple was torn in two from top to bottom. In a loud voice, Jesus called out, "Father, into your hands I commit my spirit" (Luke 23:46). That is when Jesus breathed His last. Nature put on its robe of grief because the Lord of nature had died.

A centurion, who saw the whole drama, praised God and said, "Surely this was a righteous man" (Luke 23:47).

As for me, I was still in shock. The sword of suffering had finally broken my heart and severed the earthly from the heavenly. I had lost a Son, but gained a Savior!

2

Caiaphas

"Those who had arrested Jesus took him to Caiaphas, the high priest"
(Matthew 26:57)

I knew Jesus because I condemned Him to death.

My name is Joseph Caiaphas, "the one who had advised the Jews that it would be good if one man died for the people" (John 18:14). Believe it or not, I tore my clothes when Jesus admitted He was the Son of God (Matthew 26:65).

I married the daughter of Annas, a "retired" high priest. He and I were fellow conspirators. In 6 A.D., he came to Jerusalem from Alexandria in Egypt. That's when Quirinius appointed him high priest. During that time, he established what came to be called a "dynasty" in the high priesthood.

That is, Annas was made high priest by the Roman authority. However, that was illegal because Gentile power could not designate a high priest of the Hebrew temple. After serving nine years, he retired, and his five sons succeeded him, but he still controlled things behind the scenes. Consequently, in the words of Harry Rimmer, "the destinies of the entire populace were in the hands of one man who was the general-in-chief of a standing army, treasurer of public funds and high priest of a religion which consisted of the worship of the emperor."

When Annas was seventy, he met Jesus face to face. However, being a wicked man, he was, according to Frederick W. Krummacher, " 'twice dead,' estranged from the truth of God [and] destitute of every noble feeling." In fact, he parted with ideals, lost his sense of moral values, compromised with the world, and lived for comfort rather than conviction. Klass Schilder says he "had grown gray in the service."

Annas was a true Sadducee. Galbraith Hall Todd writes, "He did not recognize the reality of the spiritual world, angels, immortality, the resurrection of the body [and] the final reckoning before the throne of God." However, he did believe in getting rid of that fanatic carpenter from Nazareth, Jesus Christ, even if he had to slay Him himself! Isn't it strange that Annas' name means "merciful"?

The Sanhedrin was the Jewish Council. It controlled the political, legislative, judicial, municipal, religious and educational departments. This council was made up of seventy-one members: twenty-three priests, twenty-three Scribes, twenty-three elders, and two presidents. Members had to meet seven requirements: wisdom, gentleness, sobriety, piety, truth, hatred for money, and perfect reputation. I was a high priest from 18 to 36 A.D., eventually becoming president.

We began questioning Jesus regarding His disciples and doctrine. We accused His disciples of belonging to a politically dangerous association. We feared their influence would threaten the Sanhedrin and our "dynasty." After all, numbers usually determine success or failure. As far as we were concerned, Jesus and His disciples were a threat. In fact, the Pharisees declared, "Look how the whole world has gone after Him!" (John 12:19). When we accused Jesus of blasphemous heresy, He replied candidly and with authority, "I have spoken openly to the world…. I always taught in the synagogues or at the temple, where all the Jews come together. I said nothing in secret. Why question me? Ask those who heard me. Surely they know what I said" (John 18:20-21). As your Gospel record says, "he taught as one who had authority, and not as their teachers of the law" (Matthew 7:29).

That's when one of the servants got up and hit Jesus in the face, asking, "Is this the way you answer the high priest?" (John 18:22). What he did not realize was that Jesus had once said, in the words of Fulton J. Sheen, "when struck we should turn the other cheek. Did He? Yes! He turned His whole body to be crucified."

The prophet Isaiah predicted: "there were many who were appalled at him–his appearance was so disfigured beyond that of any man and his form marred beyond human likeness" (Isaiah 52:14).

Why did that servant hit Jesus? It was because he really didn't understand Jesus' reply. Jesus was referring to all His teachings, practical and prophetic. However, the servant didn't understand the content. He had insulted heaven and Isaiah's Suffering Servant.

That servant did not have any authority to hit Jesus. Only Annas and I had such power, and we knew what we wanted to do with Jesus. We were the law, and Jesus was our outlaw. We would beat and insult Him inside the gate, and then crucify Him outside the gate.

Your hymn writers, Cecil Frances Humphreys Alexander and George Stebbins, put it this way:

> There is a green hill far away,
> Without a city wall,
> Where the dear Lord was crucified,
> Who died to save us all.

The logic of that impetuous servant is characteristic of us all. Often, we don't understand, but we act as though we do, simply to be in control. Consequently, the servant's blow to Christ's face has rippled in successive waves throughout the centuries. Under the direction of religious and political leaders, servants are slapping Christ right and left. They are all part of a vicious circle to hinder the Gospel. It seems that every gesture of priest or slave is to forget God, control him, or, in Schilder's words, "argue Him out of existence." It is a blow against the face of God.

As one who can say, "I told you so," listen to what your wise man, Solomon, writes: "Guard your steps when you go to the house of God. Go near to listen rather than to offer the sacrifice of fools, who do not know that they do wrong" (Ecclesiastes 5:1). In other words, as Schilder puts it, "Go cautiously, be on guard, do not let your impulse dictate your steps…do not dally in the place of seriousness, and do not play idly with sacrificial blood….”

More than ever, I saw how I had condemned Him. I was a guilty high priest, a forerunner of others who also condemn Him.

Being Annas’ son-in-law, I knew he lived a life of progressive degeneration. He lived for financial advantage…his advantage. Therefore, being part of the “dynasty,” I became well-groomed as a tyrant for Rome. Consequently, we controlled the sale of birds and animals in the Temple courts.

Each year at Passover, all Jews, both rich and poor, were expected to come to the Temple. They were required to bring a half-shekel as the price of atonement. Rimmer calls it the “shekel of the sanctuary,” and equal to the golden shekel of Galilee. However, only the shekel of the sanctuary was acceptable. So, we had the moneychangers set up their tables in the Temple court where, for a twenty percent charge, they changed foreign money into Galilean money.

On top of that, we charged a fee to inspect all the animals brought for sacrifice. Our income was enormous, making us the wealthiest around. As powerful Roman officials, we had what Rimmer calls “itching palms, which could be soothed–not cured–only by a continual application of gold. And ultimately, and always, the people paid.”

As you can tell, we had quite a thing going, at least until Jesus walked into the Temple court. When He observed the transactions, He quietly made a whip and turned into a maniac! He went through the court, slashing His whip, tipping over tables, and scattering lovers of money through every exit.

Annas and I were quite displeased. We were angry with Jesus for driving the merchants out of the Temple. We were not going to put up with it! So, we ordered Jesus’ hands to be tied, and asked the Sanhedrin to deal with Him.

The songwriter, Ray Overholt, describes it like this:

They bound the hands of Jesus in the garden where He prayed;
They led Him thro’ the streets in shame.

They spat upon the Saviour so pure and free from sin;
They said, "Crucify Him; He's to blame."

Upon His precious head they placed a crown of thorns;
They laughed and said, "Behold the King!"
They struck Him and they cursed Him and mocked His holy name
All alone He suffered everything.

To the howling mob He yielded; He did not for mercy cry.
The cross of shame He took alone.
And when He cried, "It's finished," He gave Himself to die;
Salvation's wondrous plan was done.

Can you imagine Jesus bound? Isn't that an oxymoron? How can Omnipotence be held in chains? How can the Master of the world be captured by His mortal subjects?

Do you remember your first high priest? His name was Aaron, Moses' brother. On Aaron's headdress, in letters of gold, were the words, "Holy to the Lord" (Exodus 28:36). With such a title engraved on my headdress, you would expect that I was, in Rimmer's words, "utterly incapable of doing a mean, degraded, or despicable deed."

However, the priesthood had so degenerated that the Temple had become a stronghold of an organized gang of racketeers, and I was one of the ringleaders! I know I had taken the sacred vows to direct Israel's faith and worship, but I disregarded those vows and became an apostate. The Psalmist describes me perfectly: "How long will you defend the unjust and show partiality to the wicked?.... [Y]ou will die like mere men; you will fall like every other ruler" (Psalm 82:2,7).

I assume you know what it means to be an apostate. He is one who departs from those principles which he knows are right. It's a deliberate forsaking of biblical or Christian values.

First, as an apostate, I rejected the holy law of Israel, given through Moses. Having been raised in a Palestinian family, I believed and revered the sacred law. However, I became obsessed with greed, allowing it to destroy my faith.

Second, as an apostate, I despised my priestly vows. I had made them with an honest face, but soon my heart was not in them. I became a turncoat, a hypocrite.

Third, as an apostate, I disregarded the civil law. Actually, I bent the law to suit my own purpose. I used it to plot the murder of Jesus of Nazareth. In fact, I announced that it was expedient that one man should die for the people. To do that, I allowed the Sanhedrin to overlook forty-three direct violations of the civil law. The most obvious violation was that I permitted Jesus' trial to take place at night. Besides, as John MacArthur writes, capital trials "could only be held at the Temple, and only in public."

Looking back, I knew better, but I didn't care. I became proud in my self-confidence as a politician and religionist. I was immersed in religious organizations, institutions and ceremonies. I had what your Apostle Paul calls "a form of godliness but denying its power" (2 Timothy 3:5). I had a closed mind, as Todd writes, "as fixed as an arctic winter and as unreceptive as the dead."

At Jesus' trial, we had arranged for false witnesses to testify against Him. They accused Him of planning to destroy our Temple and, in three days, build a new one. However, He was not referring to our building, but rather to His body, which they would destroy by crucifixion. He had said, "Destroy this temple, and I will raise it again in three days" (John 2:19).

In essence, He was saying, "You will destroy the temple. I know you will. I will permit you to, but in three days I will raise it up." Actually, He was predicting that they would destroy His body. So, by claiming that He said He would destroy their temple, they were guilty of falsification, the sin of false witnessing.

The truth is, Jesus was going to let His accusers destroy His body. But He was going to raise it again. That is, He must accept death by God's hand, not the hands of men. He would not use sensationalism and worldly publicity to lure people to His cross. Then, lifted to Golgotha's lofty heights, He would draw all people to Himself.

Jesus' trial turned into a question-and-answer game. The only problem was, Jesus did not answer all our questions. He remained silent, and I wondered why. Was it because He was resigned to the will of God, and would die soon anyway? Was it because He protested all the injustices of the trial? Was it because He knew His defense would not serve any purpose?

One of your poets writes:

> *The day when Jesus stood alone*
> *And felt the hearts of men like stone,*
> *And knew He came but to atone—*
> *That day "He held His peace."*
>
> *They witnessed falsely to His word,*
> *They bound Him with a cruel cord,*
> *And mockingly proclaimed Him Lord;*
> *"But Jesus held His peace."*
>
> *My friend, have you for far much less,*
> *With rage, which you called righteousness,*
> *Resented slights with great distress?*
> *Your Saviour "held His peace."*

That frustrated me to no end. We were getting nowhere. So, I instructed Jesus, "I charge you under oath by the living God: Tell us if you are the Christ, the Son of God." And Jesus answered, "Yes, it is as you say. But I say to all of you: In the future you will see the Son of Man sitting at the right hand of the Mighty One and coming on the clouds of heaven" (Matthew 26:63-64).

I wanted to know if Jesus, in His whole person, was claiming to be God's Son. Thus, by putting Him under oath, I put Him in God's presence; that is, under God's eye and accountable to Him. His answer would be judged by His Father. If He was God, God would be appealing to God.

For me, that was it. I had enough. This man must die. In fact, every time my name appears in your Bible, I am seeking Jesus' destruction.

With one voice, we all declared, "He has spoken blasphemy!.... He is worthy of death" (Matthew 26:65-66). Yes, He had blasphemed God.

He had stretched out His hands against God. He had dishonored God. Heaven will not tolerate blasphemers.

I remember it well. Jesus had declared His divinity, and I declared Him guilty of blasphemy. I was so upset and angered that I tore my garments. That was how I displayed my grief and pain. Actually, by ripping off my priestly garments, I was, in Sheen's words, bringing "an end to the priesthood of Aaron and opening the way to the priesthood of Melchisedech." My hands tore the robes of priesthood, but the hand of God would tear the veil of the Temple. I tore from bottom to top, but God tore from top to bottom.

Tearing my clothes was a symbol of grief. However, it was forbidden to priests. Priests were not to express mourning that way. They must keep their eyes on God, not on the earth. Death must not distract or detain them.

However, tearing clothes was permitted to show grief over one's blasphemy. So, when I tore my clothes, I was sharing the grief and guilt of Israel.

My torn clothes was not a symbol of my broken heart. It was a symbol of my joy over achieving the death penalty, based on our false accusations of blasphemy. My heart was as hard as ever. That was my greatest sin.

3

Pilate

"What shall I do, then, with the one you call the king of the Jews?"
Pilate asked them.
(Mark 15:12)

I knew Jesus because I sentenced Him to death.

This was in keeping with my name, Pilate, meaning, "one armed with a javelin."

Being Roman, I was appointed governor over Judea around 26 A.D., when Tiberius Caesar was emperor. I lived in Caesarea, or "little Rome," on the coast. But, when in Jerusalem, my official residence was the fortress of Antonia. On this occasion, it was Passover time, so, I had to make sure people kept the peace.

During my ten-year rule, I had a major part in the trial and death of Jesus of Nazareth. He was considered the saddest-looking figure in human history. But now, the one who sentenced Him to be nailed to the Cross is sadder still. That was me. You can be sure my name will not be associated with honor and courage. I lost both in about six hours.

Both history and your Scriptures record my notorious past. Luke says I murdered some Galileans while they offered their sacrifices (Luke 13:1). The Book of Acts has documented that, during Jesus' trial, I conspired against Him, but later tried to let Him go (Acts 4:27; 3:13). Some conclude

I was, as Friedrich August Tholuck writes, "too bad for heaven and too good for hell."

Now, thousands of years later, in cathedral and village church, earnest worshipers recite the Apostles' Creed, saying that Jesus "suffered under Pontius Pilate."

My story began when the Sanhedrin, the seventy men making up the Jewish Council, met to determine if Jesus was the Christ, the Messiah. Jesus replied, "If I tell you, you will not believe me, and if I asked you, you would not answer. But from now on, the Son of Man will be seated at the right hand of the mighty God" (Luke 22:67-69).

Then, they asked Him, " 'Are you then the Son of God?' He replied, 'You are right in saying I am' " (Luke 22:70). So, hearing Jesus' testimony, they bound Him with ropes. A few days earlier, people had shouted hosannas (Luke 19:28-44). But, on this day, the crowd surrounded Him with swords and spears, escorting Him to my residence. They wanted me to pass the death sentence on Him.

The idea of the ropes was supposed to create the impression that He had committed some awful crime. But, what they accused Him of was subverting the nation, opposing anyone paying taxes to Caesar and claiming to be Christ, a king.

When they arrived at my door, they rudely pushed Jesus into the open area of the house. If they had entered a Gentile's house, where there was leaven, they would be defiled and not allowed to eat the Passover. But, they did not care about Jesus being defiled. Of course, I saw through their hypocrisy. Imagine, being too holy to enter a Gentile's house, but committing a greater moral sin by their mistreatment of Jesus!

I went out to meet them, and, following Roman procedure, I asked Jesus, "Are you the king of the Jews?" He replied, "Yes, it is as you say" (Matthew 27:11). When the high priest heard that, he violated his own law by tearing his garments, to appeal to the jury's passions.

When I tried to establish the charge against Jesus, He remained silent. So, I told the chief priests and elders to judge Him according to their own law. But, legally, they were not allowed to put any person to death. And, the Romans could not condemn a person without a definite charge.

Besides, the Jewish authorities had a personal grievance, wanting to satisfy their envy and disregard justice. They were jealous over Jesus' popularity.

Then, the Sanhedrin reminded me it was customary to release a prisoner at Passover. So, I picked the worst criminal, Barabbas, and stood him beside Jesus. I addressed the crowd, "Do you want me to release the king of the Jews?" They shouted back, "No, not him! Give us Barabbas!" (John 18:39-40).

Barabbas was a zealot, guilty of insurrection, robbery and murder. He may have been connected to the two robbers crucified with Jesus. If so, they could have been followers of Barabbas. Consequently, Jesus literally took the place of Barabbas on the Cross.

The phrase, "Give us Barabbas," shows the degree of moral and spiritual depravity among us, and is still the request of many. Quite often, we ask, as John Calvin Reid writes, "O, how long will men defend dishonor and sin, and crucify nobility and purity? How long will the world cry, 'Give us Barabbas—money, selfishness, pleasure, personal gain, our own way—Let Jesus be crucified!' "

I was under great pressure from the people and Tiberius Caesar. In fact, the Jews made it quite clear that, "[i]f you let this man go, you are no friend of Caesar" (John 19:12). The problem was, I found no fault in Jesus. I knew He was innocent, but the people wanted Him crucified. So, I gave them their wish. But, this question still rings in my ears, "What shall I do, then, with Jesus who is called Christ?" (Matthew 27:22).

You see, I was a skeptic. And, I was shallow, without faith, which is, as Tholuck writes, "that sacred thing, which should be linked with every fibre of the human heart." I did not practice godly principles; all I had were opinions and assumptions. In fact, I wished I had the ability to withstand the people's wishes. But, as W.E. Sangster says, I preferred my "social standing to any spiritual stability."

I was on the horns of a dilemma. What was I to do…side with the people, satisfy my own conscience, or please Tiberius Caesar? The pressure was unbearable. Then, my wife, who traveled with me only by my special request, had a dream about Jesus' trial. She saw trouble and warned me not to have anything "to do with that innocent man" (Matthew 27:19).

Finally, the crowd's fanaticism turned into fury. They seemed to erupt, charging Jesus with sedition, forbidding to pay taxes to Caesar, and trying to dethrone him as king.

I knew their argument was weak, even unfounded. The charge of sedition was vague. At no time did Jesus deny the Levitical Priesthood its authority. In fact, He visited the Temple, celebrated the festivals of Israel, and obeyed the statutes of Moses.

As for paying taxes to Caesar, the authorities asked Him, "Is it right to pay taxes to Caesar or not?" But He, "knowing their evil intent," replied, "You hypocrites, why are you trying to trap me? Show me the coin used for paying the tax." When they brought it to Him, He asked, "Whose portrait is this? And whose inscription?" When they admitted it was Caesar's, He said, "Give to Caesar what is Caesar's, and to God what is God's" (Matthew 22:17-22) They had their answer and kept quiet. I knew He was right, for my officials would have informed me if Jesus had been delinquent in paying taxes.

As for the third accusation, Caesar was extremely suspicious of anyone using the name, "king." So, when some people wanted to make Jesus king, He escaped and hid from them. And, when His disciples tried to get Him to establish a kingdom, He scolded them and told them the kingdom was within them.

What was the reason for their accusations? According to Harry Rimmer, "Jesus Christ was condemned for claiming Deity." In fact, the accusers said He ought to die because He claimed to be the Son of God. To them, that was blasphemy. But, the Roman law had no such crime. Therefore, they changed the charge from blasphemy to sedition, meaning that patriotism to Judaism was sedition against Rome.

In my obvious frustration, I sarcastically asked, "What is truth?" (John 18:38). Expressing my secular heart, I was convinced the question could not be answered. I believed all religions were systems of falsehood. I figured praying people were deceived. And, I concluded the man standing before me, saying He was a king, was lying through His teeth.

My unbelief proved I "was not among those whom the Father had given to the Son," as John MacArthur writes. In fact, Jesus answered me,

"Everyone on the side of truth listens to me" (John 18:37). Admittedly, I was struggling with a moral problem I did not have the courage to solve.

Back home, we had debated it often. Since then, I have learned that, in the words of Fulton J. Sheen, "[r]ight is still right if nobody is right, and wrong is still wrong if everybody is wrong." However, in the unethical and unjust atmosphere of Jesus' trial, their truth was as good as mine. Everything was relative. All issues were subjective. There were no absolutes. Some were, as J.G. Stevenson writes, "so persuaded of their own talent for tactics that for them the crooked thing [was] always more attractive than the straight." But, as Reid adds, "I knew a certain course was right. I chose another." In fact, Tholuck dubs me as "too weak to believe in Truth, and… too weak to deny it altogether."

When that happened to me, truth and righteousness became empty words. Any eternal motives I may have had became temporal goals. The fear of flesh and blood resided where I should have had fear of God.

Actually, Jesus, the embodiment of truth, was standing right beside me, but I failed to recognize Him. I was indifferent to the truth. I didn't realize that, again in Tholuck's words, "[o]ur belief in the truth must be deliberate, certain, decided, in order that it may become a believing life!" But, I turned away from the Truth Incarnate and, in the end, was judged by it.

Then, we had a turn of events. The crowd announced that Jesus was from Galilee. *Lucky me!* I thought. *That's the territory of Herod Antipas.* So, I sent Jesus to Herod, who was in Jerusalem at that time. By the way, he is the one who had John the Baptist beheaded in prison (Matthew 14:1-12).

Surprisingly, Herod was happy to oblige. He had hoped to meet Jesus and have Him perform a miracle. So, Herod asked Him many questions, but Jesus refused to answer, even though the crowd accused Him repeatedly. Then, Herod and his soldiers mocked and ridiculed Jesus. Frustrated with the whole scene, they put Him in a kingly robe and sent Him back to me.

I then told the people Herod and I did not have any reason to charge Him. We did not believe He deserved death. So, I decided to punish Him and let Him go.

My strategy was to get sympathy for Jesus and evade all responsibility. But, I soon learned that, in Stevenson's words, "God never allows us to transfer a responsibility that is rightly ours." My plan was to chastise Jesus with a whipping or Roman lashing. But, I knew that was unfair and inhumane. After all, the court had just proclaimed Him innocent. So, to flog Him was the lowest form of degradation. On the other hand, to release Him would satisfy justice. But, can a person serve two masters? Isn't all compromise of the devil? Isn't right always right?

The whipping was cruel. MacArthur explains, "The whip used for scourging consisted of several strands of leather attached to a wooden handle. Each strand had a bit of metal or bone attached to the end. The victim was bound to a post by the wrists, high over his head, so that the flesh of the back would be taut. An expert at wielding the scourge could literally tear the flesh from the back, lacerating muscles, and sometimes even exposing the kidneys or other internal organs. Scourging alone was fatal in some cases."

I agree with the following description from Giovanni Papini: "This was the first blood drawn by men from the Son of man. At the Last Supper, His blood had been symbolized by the wine, on the Mount of Olives the blood which mixed with the sweat, stood in drops on His face, came from a suffering altogether spiritual and inner. But now, at last, men's hands shed blood from the veins of Christ; knotty hands of soldiers in the service of the rich and powerful, hands which wield the scourge before taking up the nails. That livid back, swollen and bloody, was ready for the cross; torn and raw as it was, it would add to the suffering of crucifixion when they stretched it out on the rough wood of the cross. Now they could stop, the courtyard of the cowardly stranger was stained with blood."

One of your hymn-writers, Ben H. Price, pictures it like this:

> It was alone the Savior stood
> In Pilate's judgment hall:
> Alone the crown of thorns He wore
> Forsaken thus by all.

Alone, Alone, He bore it all alone;
He gave Himself to save His own,
He suffered, bled and died alone, alone.

The law of Rome hung on this ideal, to quote Rimmer, "[t]o crush the proud and give justice to the weak." But, because of pride and the fear of others, the chief priests and elders denied this protection to the suffering Son of God. That has to be the most incredible paradox of history, a man, found innocent by the highest courts of his day, was then tortured, beaten and crucified.

Strange as it seemed to me then, in Papini's words, "Jesus had never said anything that would be offensive to Pilate.... Jesus taught love for enemies...called the poor blessed, hence He exhorted them to resignation and not to revolt. He advised men to render unto Caesar that which was Caesar's; He ate with publicans and Gentiles; and finally He announced that His kingdom was not of this world."

In my "shortsightedness, common to men of the world," as Stevenson puts it, I threw my conscience to the wind and let the people rule. I tried every trick to save the prisoner's neck but, to save my own neck, I washed my hands from the whole affair. Being innocent, and according to Jewish custom (Deuteronomy 21:6-9), I tried to absolve myself from this wrongful death. But, the general remark was, in Sangster's words, "The blood-guiltiness was on his soul."

The water that flowed over my hands was insufficient to cleanse them. My hands are still bloodstained, and will be through eternity. No washing will ever cleanse them from the stains left by Christ's divine blood. I knew there was no fault in Jesus. And, I know there is no excuse for one in authority to allow a just person to be killed.

As a result of my gruesome actions, my superiors deposed me to Gaul, and my wife banished me. Tradition says I ended my life by walking into the Rhone River and drowning myself. I am now lost and alone, with only the memory of a man, a king, who died for me.

You must be wondering what message my wife had for me. Well, as a monitor to my conscience, she tried to restrain me from the wrong course which ended in my disaster. Here, in the words of Galbraith Hall Todd, is what I got from her dream: "Let there be nothing between you and the righteous Jesus…. You cannot fight against truth and justice and right without harming your own soul. You cannot act against Christ and the ideals represented to Him without endangering your soul. Let there be no barrier of unbelief, no barrier of intellectual pride, no false hope of salvation through your own merits, no barrier of unconfessed sin between you and Jesus."

The question that still haunts me, striking a discordant note and jarring my soul, is, "What shall I do, then, with the one you call the king of the Jews?" (Mark 15:12). For me, it is too late. But, not for you. Each of you must give an account to God. What will you say on that day? What will *you* do with Jesus? If you remain undecided at death, the only appropriate symbol on your tombstone will be a question mark, not a cross or crown!

I leave you with Albert B. Simpson's question:

Jesus is standing in Pilate's hall,
Friendless, forsaken, betrayed by all;
Harken! what meaneth the sudden call?
What will you do with Jesus?

What will you do with Jesus?
Neutral you cannot be;
Some day your heart will be asking,
"What will He do with me?"

4

Herod

"Herod is going to search for the child to kill him"
(Matthew 2:13)

I knew Jesus because I tried to kill Him.

I am Herod Antipas, ruler of a fourth of Galilee. I had John the Baptist beheaded in prison (Matthew 14:1-12). It still haunts me.

I am the youngest son of Herod the Great, and a reproduction of all that is worst in his character. I am known for building the city of Tiberias, on the shores of Lake Galilee. But, most of all, I am known for having an affair with Herodias, the wife of my brother, Philip.

My family's background was Idumaean, or descendants from Esau, the father of Edom. We were killers. My father had all male children under two at Bethlehem murdered. My nephew, Herod Agrippa, killed James the Apostle. And, I sent John the Baptist to the prison I had built, according to Marcus L. Loane, "in the gloomy dungeons of Fort Machaerus," north of the Dead Sea.

When John confronted me about my affair, as Loane says, "he was not the man to put velvet in his mouth where sin was concerned." John had said, "It is not lawful for you to have your brother's wife" (Mark 6:18). My sin was a moral issue. As Loane concludes: "Moral failure is so often due to something which is cherished against the law of God."

John the Baptist was Jesus' second cousin. To me, he was, in Klass Schilder's words, "a holy and righteous man, a prophet whose credentials were indisputable." I took him seriously, even visiting him to have serious talks. I remember the good things about him. And, I knew he was right. I admit to being frivolous when I promised Herodias the head of John the Baptist on a platter. But, a promise is a promise. However, that created another memory, a dingy prison cell and John's head falling to the ground. My troubled conscience could not find rest.

As I said, John the Baptist was a good person. Many people followed and supported him. At the same time, Jesus performed miracles, attracting scores of curious onlookers. But, I was very perplexed, because some said Jesus was John, back from the dead. Or else, Jesus was Elijah. In fact, Elijah was supposed to come back and lead Israel into its messianic age (Malachi 4:5).

It really bothered me for people to believe John had come back. I had him beheaded on my birthday. So, every year, on that day, I relived it all again. If Jesus was not John, then who was He? After all, He preached the same repentance and promoted the Kingdom of God. I really wanted to meet Him.

For some reason, I knew that political craft and deception would not prevail against the spiritual. So, ever since severing John's head, I had looked over my shoulder. I was never at ease. I had feared Jesus, as I had feared John. There was still a sensitive area in my conscience. In Loane's words, I "feared Him as the guilty always fear the righteous."

I soon learned that fear is always the enemy of integrity. In fact, I quickly understood, again in Loane's words, "that conscience has a voice which must be obeyed as well as heard." And, as J.G. Stevenson writes: "If men disregard the clamors of conscience today, it will be no wonder if in the years to come…they laugh at the spiritual sensitiveness that once was theirs."

My father died in 4 B.C., when I was seventeen, the same time I became ruler of Galilee. And, since Jesus was a Galilean, Pilate thought I should question Him. It certainly wasn't Jesus' idea. He had already been tossed like a ball from Annas to Caiaphas, from Caiaphas to Pilate, and now, from Pilate to me. Besides, Pilate did not want to condemn an innocent man. So, since I was in Jerusalem for the Passover, I agreed.

I'm not sure why Pilate sent Jesus to me. After all, Pilate and I were enemies. But, as Stevenson says, "when men laugh together, enmity ceases." Yet, even though time heals all wounds, Pilate took a big risk. As it turns out, I had heard much about the "miracle worker" from Nazareth, so, I decided to check Him out. I was the third person to interview Him.

Actually, I was supposed to "try" Jesus, and hopefully accuse Him. But, I never did. All I wanted was humor. Little did I realize, again in Stevenson's words, that "[b]lasphemous humor…at the expense of sacred things is almost unpardonable." I couldn't get serious. Plus, I dreaded silence. So, I asked Jesus many questions.

Why did I react that way toward Jesus? Well, He was a cousin of John the Baptist, whom I beheaded. And, I was sure Jesus knew a lot about me. In fact, He might make me face myself. But, to my surprise, He refused to answer any of my questions. And, the more silent He became, the more my conscience replayed the face and voice of John the Baptist.

No doubt you believe the Pharisees accused me of wanting to kill Jesus. But, that is untrue. Yes, I wanted Him out of my province, for I feared His influence. But, I wouldn't dare kill Him. Besides, I honestly wanted to meet Him.

That's when Jesus called me a fox: "Go tell that fox, 'I will drive out demons and heal people today and tomorrow, and on the third day I will reach my goal' " (Luke 13:32). He might have called me a wolf, for I was merciless and thirsty for blood. He might have called me a dog, for I was as snappy and jealous as a dog with a bone. Or, He might have called me a snake, for I used slanderous words and treacherous actions. But, He called me a fox. And, He was right, for I was weak, cruel, sensual, proud and shallow-hearted. I was more fox than tiger, or any other beast. I was sly and crafty. I was a traitor, spy, murderer and adulterer, certainly not the most fitting person to condemn innocence. In no way was Jesus going to fight God's battles with Satan's weapons.

What did Jesus mean? Well, it seems He was referring to His death. That is, I could kill Him, but that would not harm Him, because He was determined to complete His work. In fact, His death would perfect His ministry. So, by going to Jerusalem to die, He would be joining a whole company of martyrs.

To me, Jesus, in Schilder's words, "showed very plainly that He goes His own way quite independently, and that He, when He is ready to enter the city which kills the prophets, will make His entry not as an embarrassed and shy candidate for the privilege of martyrdom, but as a king who follows His own schedule, and who will not be diverted from it by this old fox."

The truth is, I was certainly more guilty than Jesus. And, I was totally confused as to His identity. As James M. Stalker remarks, "A man who has no religion may yet have a great deal to say about religion…. No mouth is more voluble than that of a characterless man of feeling."

In reality, in trying to be good to the Jews, I was faithful to all their traditions, restored their Temple, and fought against Pilate's religious plunderings. And, I was in Jerusalem to attend their Passover.

I must confess my heart was heavy. I had built up much sin and guilt on my soul. My conscience was like an open wound, and it was bleeding again. I was afraid Jesus was John reincarnated. So, I was glad to see Him, because I would know for sure. Hopefully, it would remove my superstition.

When Jesus stood before me, He was bound with chains. So, I did not see Him as a danger to the public or a threat to me. In fact, when I questioned Him, He frustrated me with His silence and no-show performance.

Apparently, that was something new. John MacArthur points out that all during Jesus' trial, I was "the only one to whom He refused to speak. [Since I had] rejected the truth…from John the Baptist, so it would have been pointless for Jesus to answer [me]."

That's why I wanted a sign, a miracle. If only Jesus would perform a miracle! Just for me. It would prove me either right or wrong. But, He answered none of my questions. He held His peace. I wished someone had told me why.

Schilder explains that Jesus held His peace because He was "more than Moses…Moses performed his wonders in order to escape from the house of bondage…. But, Christ is greater than Moses. And He performs no miracle, He shows no sign, on this occasion, for the specific reason that His people will emerge from the house of bondage at the very place at which He, Christ Himself, must all alone enter into that house of bondage and be swallowed up by it."

Being more than Moses means Jesus could refuse to show a sign to benefit only Himself. After all, Jesus is still the servant of the Lord. And, He must not make Himself the purpose of His actions. Furthermore, servants must never play with signs and powers that belong to the master alone. They must find their purpose in God, the Father.

A second reason why Jesus didn't perform a miracle is that it would be in a "closed circle" only. That is, to an exclusive society only—the Scribes, chief priests, Sanhedrin and me. But, Jesus refused. He would not offer to sell spiritual goods in the markets of the unworthy.

A third reason is that my soul wasn't in it. For Jesus to respond, He needed to connect to my soul. But my fear and nervous curiosity were my worst enemies. Jesus would not satisfy my senses.

Now, from where I lift my eyes in torment, I see some of your modern churches, trying to appease people's senses rather than minister to their souls. They are catering to subjective "me-ism," while ignoring objective, concrete teaching and worship. Consequently, the Holy Spirit cannot connect to produce spiritual maturity.

Since Jesus would not entertain me with magic and miracles, I fired more questions at Him. Still, He would not respond. He knew I had gone from "fox" to "reprobate." And, I knew that when Jesus answered me nothing, my reprobation had begun. I had many opportunities to repent, but, I smothered my conscience. So, frustrated up to my teeth, I threw a white robe over His shoulders and ordered Him back to Pilate.

One of your poets has summed it up well:

> *Herod still lives and lifts the sword*
> *Of mockery against his Lord.*
> *Up Christians, rise, hear duty call,*
> *Proclaim Christ's glory unto all.*

I wasn't always a reprobate. I admit, my family background didn't help. But, it started with little immoral sins and unlawful decisions. Then, I had agreed to the murder of John the Baptist. I became like those who "did not think it worthwhile to retain the knowledge of God, [so He] gave them over to a depraved mind" (Romans 1:28).

My sensuality controlled my soul, making it impossible for God to reach me. The tree, which the storm blew over, had been rotten at the root.

My sinful life destroyed my career and marriage. I was banished to Lyons, a city in France. Historians say I died in Spain, mercilessly haunted by the memory of a head on a platter.

5

Nicodemus

*"I tell you the truth, no one can see the kingdom
of God unless he is born again"*
(John 3:3)

I knew Jesus because He showed me how to be born again.

My name is Nicodemus, a Pharisee and teacher in Israel during the ministry of Jesus of Nazareth. And, being a proud member of the Sanhedrin, the Supreme Court of the Jews, I had a purpose for living. After all, we controlled the politics and religion in Jerusalem.

In my search for truth, I heard about Jesus, and I became quite curious, especially because of His miracles. I figured He must be God-sent. And, when I heard He had turned water to wine at a wedding, I decided to visit Him. However, it had to be at night.

Why at night? Well, it wasn't because I was too busy during daylight hours. Mainly it was because I didn't want others to see me talking with Jesus. After all, He was unpopular with the Sanhedrin and most of us Pharisees. And, I could lose my membership. So, I arranged a secret visit, for a private conversation, without interruption. John Calvin Reid writes, "In all Jerusalem, I was the only rabbi to go to the trouble of seeking a personal interview with Jesus."

For Jesus to change the water into wine (John 2:1-11), I knew He had power over nature and could change external things. When He cleansed the Temple (John 2:12-25), I knew He had power over the Temple and its people to change religious rituals.

Most people will tell you I had a good life of high moral values and popular social acceptance. I was a professional, an intellectual, and extremely religious. As a Jew, I was patriotic. As a Pharisee, I was one of the "separated ones," and very dogmatic. In fact, I was, as John MacArthur writes, "highly zealous for ritual and religious purity according to the Mosaic law…. [I] represented the orthodox core of Judaism and very strongly influenced the common people of Israel." I was so zealous for the Law, some of my friends said I was "born again."

Let me explain. Arnold Fruchtenbaum writes: "To the first century Jew, 'born again' was a commonly understood term for certain rites of passage in a man's life—six different events were so labeled in Rabbinic Judaism. First was the bar mitzvah, confirming a 13-year-old boy into manhood. Second, a man was 'born again' when he married. Third, a man was 'born again' when he was ordained a rabbi. Fourth, a man was 'born again' if he became the head of a rabbinic academy. Fifth, a Gentile man was 'born again' when he converted to Judaism. And sixth, a man was 'born again' when he was crowned king."

You can imagine my confusion when Jesus declared I must be "born again" (John 3:3, 7). As far as I was concerned, I was already "born again" in at least the first four rites. I was bar mitzvahed, married, ordained, and a rabbi. But, what did Jesus mean? Would I have to become a baby and start life over?

You must understand something. Reid explains: "We rabbis were well acquainted with the doctrine of the new birth. We expounded it daily as a requirement for entering the kingdom of God—only we regarded ourselves, being 'the children of Abraham,' as already in. It was outsiders— Gentiles, publicans, and sinners—who, according to our teaching, had to be born again."

For a Pharisee, the "new birth" was radical. A second birth seemed both unnecessary and impossible. But, I had to find out how Jesus' meaning of "born again" differed from my understanding of it. So, under the cover of darkness, I met with Jesus to sort it all out.

William T. Sleeper sets the scene like this:

> *A ruler once came to Jesus by night*
> *To ask Him the way of salvation and light;*
> *The Master made answer in words true and plain,*
> *"Ye must be born again."*

Apparently, Jesus knew my curiosity and need. For, plainly and abruptly, He said, "no one can see the kingdom of God unless he is born again" (John 3:3). He knew my own "born-again" experiences, but He insisted I needed to be born "from above" (John 3:31). That would give me new life here and eternal life in the Kingdom of God. Remember, I was a supernaturalist who, in MacArthur's words, "naturally and eagerly expected the coming of the prophesied resurrection of the saints and institution of the messianic kingdom."

But, how would this happen? How could I be "born again" spiritually? Jesus said it was by "water and the Spirit" (John 3:5); that is, spiritual cleansing and renewal activated by God's Spirit. If I looked to Jesus to purify my soul, God would grant me regeneration and eternal life. To explain it further, Jesus used the "uplifted serpent" as an example (John 3:14). A serpent was lifted on a pole—Jesus was lifted on a cross. In fact, the snake-bitten Israelites had to look at the serpent on the pole to live (Numbers 21:8). So, I must look to Jesus, believe in His sacrifice, and commit my will to Him.

Some of your New Testament writers explain that since Adam and Eve sinned, all of us lost our relationship with God (Romans 5:12; 1 Corinthians 15:21). So, a new start, regeneration or rebirth, is needed. That new birth makes a person a new creation of God, born again of His Spirit.

In other words, God breathes new life into people, making them alive unto Him (Ephesians 2:1-5). As Andrew Culverwell writes,

> *Born again, there's really been a change in me!*
> *Born again, just like Jesus said.*

Born again, and all because of Calvary—
I'm glad, so glad, that I've been born again!

For me, that would really take a miracle. After all, it was more than the popular slogan many make of it today. I saw it as a change of heart towards God. It required me to renounce my religious merits, such as observing holy days and upholding the Mosiac Law. As well, I would have to give up my social status with the Sanhedrin. But, since I could not do this on my own, I would need a divine miracle.

To me, Jesus' miracles confirmed what He said. He claimed to speak God's word, and Jesus' miracles proved it. I could tell that only He could work miracles. Satan can work magic tricks, but he is only a creature. Sure, he can deceive, but he can be only in one place at a time. His fallen angels do his itinerary work.

I soon learned that Jesus did not produce miracles to win a crowd. Rather, He did miracles to prove His Word and confirm its message.

From your perspective, I was lukewarm. I gave my heart only halfway. I wanted to follow Jesus, but not in public. I wished to be "born again," but I was a coward. Like Joseph of Arimathea, I became a secret disciple (John 19:38). But, as J. Sidlow Baxter explains, "The only Christian discipleship which really overjoys the heart is that which is open, public, unashamed." Tradition says Peter baptized me, and I was put to death for becoming a believer.

Looking back at it now, Jesus was trying to show me what Carrie E. Breck writes:

There was One who was willing to die in my stead,
That a soul so unworthy might live;
And the path to the cross He was willing to tread,
All the sins of my life to forgive.

John, one of your Gospel writers, records that I once stood up for Jesus (John 7:50-52). The story is this: as a member of the Sanhedrin, the Jewish Council, and a teacher of the Jews, I knew and taught the Law. So, I questioned why we condemned Jesus before we heard His side of the case. In fact, we were not allowed to condemn Him in His absence. The Rabbinic law states: "Flesh and blood may pass judgment on a man if it hears his words; if it does not hear them, it cannot establish its judgment." On that point, Roman and Jewish law agree.

Six months later, I helped Joseph of Arimathea prepare Jesus' body for burial (John 19:38-42). We were not next of kin, but Pilate released Jesus' body for Him to have a Jewish burial. Unlike the Romans, who would leave bodies on crosses, Jewish law specified that corpses must not be left on crosses on the Sabbath. So, the crucified had to be buried before sunset.

Working with a little glow from our night torches, we could barely see what we were doing. The only Light which could dispel the darkness was dead. But, the whiteness from the Hill of the Skull glimmered on the naked corpses. We could see the long streaks of blood which ran down the crosses and soaked into Golgotha's soil. All I could think about was Moses' serpent on a pole.

First, as gently as possible, we removed the nail holding Jesus' feet. Then, one of our helpers climbed a ladder and slowly extracted the nails from His hands. At the same time, he draped Jesus' body over his shoulder and lowered it to the ground.

If you had been behind the scenes watching us, very likely you would have sung John Newton's hymn:

> *I saw One hanging on a tree,*
> *In agony and blood,*
> *Who fixed His languid eyes on me,*
> *As near His cross I stood.*
>
> *O, can it be, upon a tree,*
> *The Savior died for me?*
> *My soul is thrilled, my heart is filled,*
> *To think He died for me.*

Amazingly, Jesus' body did not have a single broken bone. His death could not be hastened. He must die voluntarily. Besides, His body had a future. So, His Father spared Him all meaningless suffering.

We then made our way to Joseph's garden, where he had built a new tomb for himself and his family. It was ideal, because it was nearby and new. By tradition, as Klass Schilder writes, "an altar was placed on new stones, the holy things were set on a new vehicle…and…holy salt was placed in a new container." So, it was fitting that Jesus have a new grave.

With the help of some servants, we washed His body, especially His wounds, and tenderly removed the crown of thorns and washed His matted hair. It reminded me of the time He had washed His disciples' feet.

After washing off dust, blood and sweat, we sprinkled His body with seventy-five pounds of myrrh and aloe spices. We also spread the spices on linen strips, which we tightly wrapped around the body.

Why so many spices? First, being two of the richest men in Jerusalem, we could afford it (Matthew 27:57). Second, since Pilate called Jesus "the King of the Jews" (John 19:19), we figured He should have a royal burial. But, most importantly, we gave Him such care because we loved and believed in Him. And, based on His promise to rebuild his "temple" (John 2:19), we expected Him to rise again. We knew we would bury Him but once.

I must quickly point out that our corpse had not requested fine linens. He did not care for myrrh, aloes and luxurious perfumes imported from abroad. But, as our "guarantee of a better covenant" (Hebrews 7:22), He would make sure He endured as a satisfactory payment for our sin.

Finally, we placed His body in a low cubicle in the tomb and sang a mortuary psalm. Then, as silently as possible, we crept out of the tomb and moved a great stone across the doorway.

Our duty done and our conscience eased, we headed home in the gathering darkness, awaiting the next miracle.

6

John the Beloved

"The disciple whom Jesus loved"
(John 21:20)

I knew Jesus because I sat next to Him at the supper table.
I am known as "the disciple whom Jesus loved" (John 13:23; 19:26; 20:2; 21:7, 20). But, don't let that fool you. I have my weaknesses, which show I am not a saint, as some think. Nor am I an intellectual. I am an ordinary man (Acts 4:13).

I lived with my parents, Zebedee and Salome, and my twin brother, James. He and I did not attend rabbinical schools. We grew up learning from experience, exploring life and being mischievousness. I was curious and intuitive.

My father was a fisherman, and James and I fished with him. That is, until one day, while we were cleaning our nets, Jesus came by and called us to follow Him. He wanted to make us "fishers of men" (Matthew 4:19). As Jesus' disciples, we were both followers and learners. However, being apostles meant we had authority (1 Thessalonians 2:6).

I was pleased when Jesus chose us to be His disciples. He knew our potential and background as successful fishermen. We weren't poor, but we were used to life's extras, like household servants. Of course, we were also familiar with what the world had to offer.

I admit it, James and I were radicals. By following Jesus, we may be able to change the establishment. Mark records that I was intolerant. "Teacher," I said, "we saw a man driving out demons in your name and we told him to stop, because he was not one of us." But, Jesus said, "Do not stop him. No one who does a miracle in my name can in the next moment say anything bad about me, for whoever is not against us is for us" (Mark 9:38-39). By that rebuke, Jesus taught an important lesson: that man and I were, in Archibald MacLeish's words, "both fighting on the same side."

I could see that, as Merrill C. Tenney points out, I "needed Jesus' counsel as much as any other of the twelve, for [James and I] seem to have possessed unusually ardent temperaments."

Besides our intolerance, we had a temper. That's why Jesus labeled us Boanerges, "Sons of Thunder" (Mark 3:17). Some Samaritans stopped Jesus and His disciples from entering their village. Knowing that Elijah had done something similar (2 Kings 1:9-15), James and I suggested calling fire from heaven to burn up their village. We were angry and wanted revenge. But, this reminded me that, before I could become the "Apostle of Love," I had to control my unruly temper. So, Jesus simply rebuked us (Luke 9:55).

Before you quickly condemn us, let me inform you that we were rather ambitious. We aspired to advance and be part of Jesus' inner circle. You can't fault us for that, can you?

Here's what happened. We were on our way to Jerusalem with Jesus and His disciples when we proposed, "Teacher, we want you to do for us whatever we ask." Jesus inquired, "What do you want me to do for you?" We replied, "Let one of us sit at your right and the other at your left in your glory" (Mark 10:35-37). Jesus bluntly told us we didn't know what we were asking. He advised us that His followers must be baptized with His baptism of suffering, but positions in glory have already been assigned.

As part of Jesus' inner circle, He took us, along with Peter, to pray with Him in the Garden of Gethsemane (Mark 14:32-42). He wanted us to share the agony of His soul as He solicited His Father's help. As we had shared His glory on the Mount of Transfiguration (Mark 9:2-13), so we would share His severe grief in His supreme crisis. As He prayed, He was very heavy with sorrow—losing all vigor and feeling extreme anguish.

Personally, I had three good years as Jesus' friend. In fact, I witnessed such momentous events as the raising of Jairus' daughter (Mark 5:35-43), Jesus' dazzling glory on the Mount (Matthew 17:2), and His agony in the Garden, when His sweat was like drops of blood (Luke 22:44).

The most moving scene for me was when Jesus, taking a towel and basin of water, washed the feet of each disciple. He filled the role of a slave and, by example, showed us that "no servant is greater than his master" (John 13:16).

As the beloved disciple (John 21:20), I was, in Henry Lockyer's words, "the disciple whom Jesus kept on loving. I was the disciple who best loved Jesus."

In His dying moments on the Cross, Jesus trusted me enough to commit His mother to me. He said to her, "Dear woman, here is your son," and to me, "Here is your mother" (John 19:26-27). But, why me? Well, Jesus and I enjoyed a "best-friend" relationship. He could not depend on His own brothers, because they were unbelievers and absent at the time. Besides, from now on, Jesus would be building His Church, which would be, in the words of Charles F. Pfeiffer and Everett F. Harrison, "spiritual rather than natural."

When you read the Book of Acts, you will not find me calling down judgmental fire from heaven. Instead, I will be laying hands on believers, to receive the fire of the Holy Spirit (Acts 8:15).

I was pleased to witness Jesus' ascension (Acts 1:9-13). Again, Pfeiffer and Harrison write, "The ascension of Christ meant that He had broken off visible fellowship with His disciples on earth, and, still bearing His resurrected body, had entered the invisible world of God's dwelling."

I remember when Jesus predicted Peter's martyrdom. Peter enquired as to what would happen to me. Was he really concerned for me or jealous of me? All Jesus said to him was, "You must follow me" (John 21:22). In other words, Peter was not to be anxious about me, but about his own devotion to Jesus and the Gospel. Just as I had been Jesus' faithful follower, Peter must follow my example.

You may have heard I wrote the Gospel of John, the Book of Revelation, and the three Epistles of John. I wrote the Gospel so my readers would "believe that Jesus is the Christ, the Son of God, and that by believing you may have life in his name" (John 20:31). I wrote Revelation to show how Satan opposes the establishment of Christ's kingly rule, but that Christ will be victorious over Satan's evil forces. I wrote the epistles to encourage you to practice love, walk in truth, and have eternal life by believing on the name of the Son of God.

The Holy Spirit inspired me to write my epistles during days of unrest, uncertainty and persecution. I wanted you to know what you can know for sure. You don't need to suppose, assume or hope so. When I said, "We know" (1 John 2:3), it was a genuine conviction. None of us can live on doubts and negatives. To have a positive purpose in life, we need a positive "know-so" faith in Christ.

In using the phrase "We know," I was confident of three truths.

First, I was positive of holiness. I knew this because "anyone born of God does not continue to sin; the one who was born of God keeps him safe, and the evil one cannot harm him" (1 John 5:18).

Second, I was so positive of regeneration, I declared, "We know that we are children of God, and that the whole world is under the control of the evil one" (1 John 5:19). Third, I was positive of Christ's deity. I proudly affirmed, "We know also that the Son of God has come and has given us understanding, so that we may know him who is true. And we are in him who is true—even in his Son Jesus Christ. He is the true God and eternal life" (1 John 5:20).

As you can tell, I was a witness for Christ. I both knew Him and had faith in Him. I saw His miracles. I heard Him teach, and I meditated on these things. I can tell the world, "I know these things are true."

In my old age, I was banished to the barren island of Patmos, south of Ephesus. There, one Lord's day—your Sunday—I was "in the Spirit" (Revelation 1:10). That is, I was supernaturally taken out of this world, to experience another world, where God gave me visions of the Church's future and God's glory in eternity.

7

Peter

"Then Peter remembered the word the Lord had spoken to him:
'Before the rooster crows today, you will disown me three times'"
(Luke 22:61)

I knew Jesus because I denied Him.

My full name is Simon Peter, from Capernaum. I was known as Simon before I knew Jesus, and Peter, the "Rock," after I knew Him.

My sanguine personality was impressionable, fickle, impulsive, boastful, self-confident and unreliable. I always seemed to live on uneven ground. I was either on the mountain or in the valley. I liked the pleasant, not the controversial, side of life. When I became irritated, it was mostly with myself. My wife can testify to that.

My brother, Andrew, and I were fishermen. He introduced me to Jesus, whom I found to be a man's man. I was impressed. But, before Jesus called me to follow Him, I was profane and unstable. I wondered why He chose me. Yet, after I became His disciple, I gave Him my life. At times, I was weak, but never a hypocrite. Even when I denied Jesus, I still loved Him. And, I knew He loved me.

My invitation to be Jesus' disciple was simple and pointed. Andrew and I were fishing on Lake Galilee, when Jesus saw us throwing a net overboard. He called, "Come, follow me, and I will make you fishers of men" (Matthew 4:19). So, we quit fishing and followed Him. Just like that.

That was the beginning of my exciting and eventful life. The first miracle I saw was Jesus feeding the five thousand with five loaves and two fish. Then, He told us to get into the boat and cross the lake. During the night, strong winds and high waves battered our vessel. We were terrified, especially when we saw a "ghost." But, it was Jesus walking on the water. After He calmed our fears, I said, "Lord, if it's you, tell me to come to you on the water." He replied, "Come" (Matthew 14:28-29). So, I jumped over the side and walked on the water towards Him. When I took my eyes off Him, though, I began to sink. Fortunately, I called to Him, and He rescued me.

Another incident happened in Caesarea Philippi, where Jesus asked us who we thought He was. Without hesitation, I declared, "You are the Christ, the Son of the living God." That's when He called me "blessed," and gave me "the keys of the kingdom of heaven" (Matthew 16:15-17, 19).

I remember also Jesus telling us He was going to Jerusalem, where He would be killed, but raised on the third day. I became furious and told Him, "Never, Lord! This shall never happen to you!" However, He rebuked me, saying, "Get behind me, Satan! You are a stumbling block to me; you do not have in mind the things of God, but the things of men" (Matthew 16:21-23).

My greatest thrill was to be on the Mount of Transfiguration with Jesus, James and John. After chatting with Moses and Elijah, Jesus displayed His glory. I was so excited, I exclaimed, "Lord, it is good for us to be here. If you wish, I will put up three shelters—one for you, one for Moses and one for Elijah." But, a voice from the cloud said, "This is my Son, whom I love; with him I am well pleased. Listen to him" (Matthew 17:1-5).

Sometime later, I got the shock of my life. Jesus predicted I would soon disown Him, saying, "this very night, before the rooster crows, you will disown me three times" (Matthew 26:34). However, I assured Him that, even if I had to die, I would never disown Him.

So, what would lead me to deny Jesus? For one thing, it wasn't sudden. It had been gradually building for a long time. One of your Christian scholars, Klass Schilder, describes it like this: "The polluted springs welling up out of the dark recesses of Peter's heart had long been active in their subterranean abodes. Peter's sin in denying the Christ had been conceived in his soul long before this moment in which it was born."

No doubt, you remember reading about Jesus' offer to wash my feet. Why do you think He wanted to do that? Was it, in the words of Frederick W. Krummacher, to "appear in his dignity? To display the splendor of his divine glory? To constrain his disciples to bow the knee in the dust before him?" No, He did it to identify with us and humble Himself as our menial servant.

But, I refused at first. Not because I didn't need cleansing, but because I thought I should wash His feet. So, I resisted.

If you will recall, resistance was my history. I resisted Jesus going to Jerusalem to die. I resisted Him when He wanted to wash my feet. But, my resistance got me nowhere, other than souring my relationship with Jesus and stunting my spiritual growth.

I began to see that I was a coward. True, I singlehandedly grabbed a sword and faced the Roman soldiers in Gethsemane. But, all I did was to substitute a swinging sword for spirituality. While I made progress in effort, I soon began to make "progress in error," to quote Harry Rimmer. I discovered that my courage was not in the faithfulness of Jesus, but entirely in my self-confidence, which I had exaggerated in my loyalty. That brought my denial and downfall.

Having learned my lesson, let me assure you, again in Rimmer's words: "If we yield to Satan once, it is easier to do so again." As John Calvin Reid points out, "The lesson for you is that old habits of sin are hard to kill. No matter how long you may have followed Christ, the evil which was part of you before you knew Him is buried in the depths of your subconscious, waiting for an opportunity to leap forth and to express itself in some new and awful form. This is the penalty for days given to sin. The man who has been a drunkard, an adulterer, a liar, or a user of profanity will always have to keep careful watch over the graveyard of his past."

You may have trouble believing this but, wanting to be part of the crowd, I failed Jesus in His greatest hour of need. I became a coward. I denied Him while He was on trial. And, that's a common sin today. That is, being a weak witness when there's a need for a positive answer to the definite question, "Do you belong to Christ?"

As I see it, there is no such thing as a free agent. We are friends of either the world or Christ. We are agents for Satan or Christ. We are under the power of Satan or God.

The One whom I denied was more than a man. He was God's Son, my Lord, Master and Redeemer. He gave His life a ransom for me. He washed my feet. We shared the Communion cup. Yet, I disowned Him, shaming Him in the eyes of His generation. I had once confessed that He is the Son of the living God but, in Gethsemane, I called Him simply a "man" (Matthew 26:72). However, the fact is, I still belonged to Him. His love had not changed. I knew that "God's solid foundation stands firm, sealed with this inscription: 'The Lord knows those who are His' " (2 Timothy 2:19). You express it in Annie J. Flint's song:

> His love has no limit, His grace has no measure,
> His power no boundary known unto men;
> For out of His infinite riches in Jesus
> He giveth, and giveth, and giveth again.

The story of how I denied Jesus started with my own spiritual downfall. I neglected to pray. The disciples and I were in the Garden of Gethsemane. Jesus asked us to pray with Him, but we fell asleep. Then, when His enemies came to arrest Him, we left Him to move towards what Schilder calls the "deeper abysses of affliction."

Isn't it awful what happens when we neglect prayer? I was vanquished and frustrated, and hell was happy.

The second step in my downfall came when I associated with the wrong crowd, the enemy. Consequently, I followed Jesus "at a distance" (Matthew 26:58). That's when I moved closer to His enemies, not to look like them, but to refrain from having to confess Him. I wasn't aware that "[b]ad company corrupts good character" (1 Corinthians 15:33). In time, I was so cornered regarding my relationship with Jesus that I denied it with oaths and curses, exclaiming, "I don't know the man!" (Matthew 26:72).

The more I followed "at a distance," the more comfortable I was with the enemy. I saw that, to quote Fulton J. Sheen, "[a]ny distance from the sun of righteousness is darkness."

According to Rimmer, "A vast majority of the church of Jesus Christ… are doing that identical thing today…and are putting themselves in places of danger." They often sit around the campfires of Jesus' enemies, where the language and conversation put them in the minority, and their faith goes silent.

The third step in my downfall was lying and profanity. Reid writes: "It was the backwash of my sinful past…[and] an old habit of bygone days when I was a fisherman on the Lake of Galilee."

If I had known it, I could have related well to Charles Wesley's lines,

Just and holy is Thy name;
I am all unrighteousness;
False and full of sin I am,
Thou art full of truth and grace.

My lies were blatant, brazen and bare-faced. And, that led to perjury, which includes the sin of blasphemy, when I cursed and swore that I didn't know Jesus. I deliberately took His name in vain, thoughtlessly driving Him to taste what Schilder calls "the bitterness of absolute isolation."

That early April night was cold. John and I entered the courtyard, to witness Jesus' trial. A group of soldiers had kindled a fire, so I joined them to warm myself. Momentarily, the High Priest's maid, who guarded the door, approached me and said, "You also were with Jesus of Galilee." But, I denied it, saying, "I don't know what you're talking about" (Matthew 26:69-70).

I headed for the door, to make my escape. But, it was not to be, for another girl announced to the soldiers, "This fellow was with Jesus of Nazareth." Again, I denied it, saying, "I don't know the man" (Matthew 26:71-72).

I tried to evade any further public contact. However, after an hour, a fresh crowd surrounded me and exclaimed, "Surely you are one of them, for your accent gives you away" (Matthew 26:73).

That was it. I'd had enough. But, I was trapped. What should I do? Admit that they were right, or continue my denial? I decided to be like one of them. So, I resorted to my old sailor-fisherman character and, with heavy curses, swore, in no uncertain terms, that I did not know Jesus!

Isn't it unusual that two women provoked my first two denials? It goes to show that women must be doubly alert when dealing with men like me. And, men, so impulsive and unreliable as me, can be very weak under female influence.

The crowing of a rooster suddenly jarred me to my senses. I remembered Jesus' prediction about my denial (Matthew 26:34). Turning, I saw Jesus, being led away. Hearing the rooster, He knew I had fallen. So, He turned, and our eyes met, the Savior and the sinner. And, in seeing Him, I saw myself, as Reid writes, "a liar, deserter, a traitor, a yellow coward."

But, I saw Jesus, too. I saw His heart, without anger. Pain without indignation. Disappointment, yet also love and forgiveness. I saw the kind of person I had denied. And, it broke my heart, moving me to repentance. I recalled what the Psalmist had written: "The sacrifices of God are a broken spirit; a broken and contrite heart, O God, you will not despise" (Psalm 51:17).

At that moment, I remembered Jesus' other prediction: "Simon, Simon, Satan has asked to sift you as wheat. But I have prayed for you, Simon, that your faith may not fail. And when you have turned back, strengthen your brothers" (Luke 22:31-32). Jesus knew I was going to fail, but He would not fail me. His faith in me was not exhausted. His love would not let me go. He would forgive me and use me in His service. If I had only known George Matheson's hymn, I would have heartily sung:

> O Love that will not let me go,
> I rest my weary soul in thee;
> I give thee back the life I owe,
> That in thine ocean depths its flow

May richer, fuller be.

By this time, my fellow disciples had run from the Garden. Their actions seemed to say, "We know him, yet, we can't watch what will happen to him." But, I chose to lie and declare, "I don't know him. I don't belong to him." In that way, I was saying, as Schilder writes, "His future does not affect me; His problem is no concern of mine; all this commotion about the Nazarene leaves me cold." So, I stayed and warmed myself by the enemies' fire.

In reflection, let me explain the turning point in my downfall. It was Jesus' look. In His face, I saw pain and suffering. I saw the dew and sweat of Gethsemane's agony. I saw a face, bloody from the blows of His enemies. I saw a face of love and compassion for me. Then, my tears of repentance poured down my face. And, I thought to myself, "Yes, Lord, you know that I love you" (John 21:17).

The look on Jesus' face broke my resistance, and I wept openly. I was truly sorry. I wanted to be a new man, His man. So, I repented, knowing that, in Sheen's words, "[r]epentance is not concerned with consequences." Repentance means that, in the light of God's grace, I passed judgment on my sin. Repentance led me back to God, where I began to live in hope again.

In my weakness, I had used cursing to endorse my lying. I thought nothing would break me; nothing, that is, until Jesus glanced at me. I had lied and denied, and all He did was look at me. I melted as I wept into the night.

Why did Jesus tolerate my denial? Krummacher's answer is: "His heart was not to be a stranger to any grief or pain, in order that he might be to us in all things a compassionate High Priest."

The lesson you can learn from this is, to quote Randal Earl Denny, "We must not be quick to judge Peter. It is wrong to give up on a fellow because he fails in one critical hour. Soon Peter will be filled with the Spirit of God at the festival of Pentecost and thousands will be converted to Jesus Christ."

In closing, let me say that God has many voices to awaken and convict us of our sin. But, our sinful life is opposed to His voice. And, in our spiritual struggle, our attention capacity is slow to respond. For me, God used a rooster, His feathered watchman, as His alarm clock. God opened the beak of the fowl, Christ opened His eyes, and I opened my heart.

8

John Mark

*"The owner of the house…will show you a large upper room,
furnished and ready. Make preparations for us there."*
(Mark 14:14-15)

I knew Jesus because I prepared the guest room for His Passover supper.

It pleased the Holy Spirit to conceal my name and genealogy. So, you can only guess at my identity.

Consequently, Jesus didn't use my Christian name. He knew I must remain unknown. However, most people believe I am John Mark, who lived with my mother, Mary, in Jerusalem.

As one of Jesus' secret followers, I belonged to a Christian underground network in Jerusalem. But, on this occasion, I am a host, "the owner of the house" (Mark 14:14). As such, you remember me for what I did for Jesus.

And what was that? Well, I was involved with the Last Supper, the Passover Feast. In fact, as I watched Jesus celebrate that Feast, I knew His love and felt His sorrow. I even heard someone say they would betray Him. I saw Judas leave the room. Afterwards, I followed Jesus to Gethsemane and listened to His prayer of agony. I watched as Judas and the soldiers arrested Him. The whole scene was quite sad and traumatic!

It took great courage to go through it all, but I felt courageous. I knew cowards don't last long on the spiritual journey. Besides, most people called Jesus a heretic. And, I was fully aware that the Supreme Court, the Sanhedrin, desired to put Him on trial. But, as Jesus' friend, I wanted the Passover celebrations to go as smoothly as possible. So, I provided the food: herbs, sauce, spices, fruit, grape juice and unleavened bread. And, I prepared a large room, with a table, mats and couches. I even arranged for the lamb to be sacrificed and roasted.

Imagine, Jesus, my Passover Lamb, came to *my* house for His Passover! He came as the great Son of David and asked for a room in his city. He came as the mediator of the New Covenant, with one great desire, to "eat the Passover with [his] disciples" (Mark 14:14).

Why a Passover? Why a lamb? Why a substitute's blood? Because the Passover lamb represented all of Jesus' sufferings. It was a sign of God's exceeding love and the satisfaction for His holiness. Undoubtedly, when Jesus saw that lamb, it shocked His soul, reminding Him of His own death. But, He had to die. His own blood would open the way to God. At the same time, the Passover was the symbol of Israel's secured deliverance.

In other words, God was there! This is how one of your own writers, G. Stuart McWhirter, puts it: "In the last century, Holocaust survivor Elie Wiesel tells of an awful encounter with the rawest evil and darkest human depravity when he was a prisoner at Auschwitz. Another Jewish prisoner was being executed while the rest of the camp was forced to watch. As the prisoner hung on the gallows, struggling in the throes of death and refusing to die, an onlooker muttered under his breath with increasing desperation, 'Where is God? Where is He?' From out of nowhere, Wiesel exclaimed, a voice within him spoke to his own heart, 'Right there on the gallows; where else?' Wiesel was right, God was on the gallows at Auschwitz. And God was naked and nailed to a Roman cross at Golgotha."

For as long as I can remember, I was interested in Jesus and His helpers. As a young man, I traveled with Paul and Barnabas to Perga. In fact, I accompanied my Uncle Barnabas, a Levite, to the island of Cyprus, his birthplace. Your Scriptures call him "Son of Encouragement" (Acts 4:36). Later, I was with Paul during his first Roman imprisonment, and also with Peter in Babylon. But, one highlight I will never forget is the prayer meeting we held in our home for Peter's release from prison. I became both a close friend of Peter and a faithful follower of Jesus.

As you know, Jesus had public acquaintances and personal friends, some of whom traveled openly with Him. But not me. I was the secret agent. I was like an unsigned letter or initials in a diary. In fact, you will recognize some of our group: Nicodemus, Joseph of Arimathea, the woman who anointed Jesus' feet, Simon of Cyrene who carried Jesus' cross, and the soldier who lifted a wet sponge to His parched lips.

No doubt many of you belong to that secret following. Where and when you met Jesus is very significant for you. Indeed, one of your unknown authors has written:

> If we cannot tell HOW we met God,
> If we cannot show WHERE we met God,
> If we cannot express why we LOVE God,
> If we cannot explain when we FEEL God,
> If we cannot describe what God MEANS to us,
> Then perhaps we have raised an altar to an "unknown God."

But, you were instantly and irresistibly attracted to Him. You had a genuine affection for each other. And, over the years, you have developed a deep friendship, a sweet fellowship and a strong faith. You now belong to each other for time and eternity.

An anonymous poet puts it this way:

> *The stars look up to God.*
> *The stars look down on me.*
> *The stars shine over the earth, and*
> *The stars shine over the sea.*
> *The stars will shine for a million years,*
> *For a million years and a day;*
> *But Christ and I will live and love*
> *When the stars have passed away.*

I can see it as though it were yesterday. Early on the day of the Passover, Jesus told Peter and John to go into the city. There, they would meet a man, with a large jug of water on his shoulder. He would lead them to a house suitably prepared, not a makeshift place. As Klass Schilder writes, "God in His providence supplied an apartment whose atmosphere and convenience suited the sanctity of the purpose." That is, everyone must be able to eat in safety and freedom. In fact, Jesus' heart must be, as Herbert F. Stevenson puts it, "at leisure from itself [and] utterly devoted to the concerns of His kingdom, and of His disciples." To Him, this was His messianic purpose, which would reverberate down through the centuries.

Jesus knew when and where He would celebrate the Passover. By His infallible knowledge, He knew my mother Mary and me. He knew where we lived, and He knew the man carrying the jug of water. In fact, this water-jug was Jesus' secret code, to hide the location from Judas as long as possible. The point is, women carried water-jugs, while men carried waterskins. Tomorrow it would be unlawful to carry anything. So, this secret would give Jesus control over the Passover meal. Besides, devout Jews must respect their night of deliverance from Egypt. So, Jesus honored them by controlling their special mealtime. And, if He could control His own death, then surely He can be trusted to sustain us in our final hour.

In my estimation, the message of the New Testament is that God is not removed from our agony. Rather, because He shares our agony, we may share His victory over evil and death at Calvary. John R.W. Stott writes: "I could never believe in God, if it were not for the cross."

As the house owner, what mattered was what I did for Jesus, and the spirit in which I did it. One of your own authors, Francois Fenelon, explains it this way: "The smallest things become great when God requires them of us; they are small only in themselves; they are always great when they are done for God, and when they serve to unite us with Him eternally."

Incidentally, do you know the difference between duty and thought? Duty acts only on command, while thought responds to the heart. Duty goes the first mile, because one is ordered to do so; thought goes the second mile because of love. For example, the dutiful child finishes the chore and runs off to play. But, the thoughtful child asks, "Mother, is there anything else I can do?" In other words, dutifulness is the cup of obedience filled to the brim. Thoughtfulness is that same cup running over!

So, I speak from experience. I gave my furnished upper room to the Master because of love. When He said, "If you love me, you will obey what I command" (John 14:15), I knew that love must always outrun duty. I distinctly remember Jesus' last week in Jerusalem. The rulers and chief priests tried to ensnare Him in His talk. The gossipers argued about His claim to be the Son of God. And, His disciples wondered when His kingdom would appear, selfishly debating who would be the greatest in it.

The truth is, I was honored to prepare that room for Jesus' Passover. I appreciated being there to hear Him say, "This is my body, which is for you." I can still see Him lifting the cup as He explained, "This cup is the new covenant in my blood" (1 Corinthians 11:24-25). In fact, phrases like "I am the vine; you are the branches" (John 15:5) and "[d]o not let your hearts be troubled" (John 14:1) melodiously ring in my ears! And, to think that Jesus spoke those words on a Thursday night, in the upper room of my house!

After the meal, before leaving for the Mount of Olives, we all sang the Jewish Hallel, Psalm 116-118. Then, we went out and disappeared into what Stevenson calls the "blackest night of all history."

That's when it struck me…that room was holy ground! I saw the couch where Jesus had reclined. I touched the table and His cup. Israel's greatest teacher, my Master, had been in my house. It seemed His presence still lingered. I felt as though I could hear His tender voice. He ate His last Passover and instituted the Lord's Supper in my upper room. Then, He set His face towards Calvary, to die for the sins of the world, even where you live.

Do you know why? Why the Cross? Why the suffering? Because, as McWhirter writes, "only God incarnate, in His own person, can face the very worst that evil and suffering have ever done upon earth."

From that moment, I made sure my room would be His room, kept for Him and His friends. Indeed, I like to think that, after His death and burial, His disciples returned to my upper room. And, the women, on that resurrection morning, hurried there. Cleopas and his companion rushed there, all the way from Emmaus, to tell how the risen Lord had broken and shared bread with them. And, Jesus appeared in that room and said, "Peace be with you!" A week later, Jesus came again and, showing His hands and side to Thomas, said, "Put your finger here; see my hands. Reach out your hand and put it into my side. Stop doubting and believe" (John 20:26-27). And, to think, that happened in my house.

Don't misunderstand me. I'm not boasting. But, I am trying to provoke you to a holy jealousy. Why? Because you may do what I did. You can give Him a large room—your heart. He has been rejected long enough. Tragedy of tragedies, many hearts and homes still do not welcome Him! They keep Him outside, while they spurn His love and argue about His justice. But, to those who make room for Him, He will become, in the words of a popular plaque, the "unseen guest at every meal and the silent listener to every conversation."

As you know, I gave Jesus a room in my house. It was an upper room, like a veranda or patio on the roof. It was secluded, away from the noise of the street. And, it was elevated and open to the stars. Cool, refreshing breezes blew away the heat of the day and brought peace during the damp nights.

My room was also equipped with furniture, food, water, basin and fresh towels. It wasn't lavish, but adequate and in good taste, furnished with what Jesus needed. I had to make it available that day. Tomorrow, when Jesus would be on the Cross, would not be good enough. So, when His disciples asked, "Where is the guest room, where I may eat the Passover with my disciples?" (Luke 22:11), my room was ready.

That night in Jerusalem was my night, for what Jesus said included me. His promise was, "In my Father's house are many rooms…. I am going there to prepare a place for you…. I will come back and take you to be with me" (John 14:2-3). In effect, He was saying, "I am your guest tonight, but soon, you will be my guest. You and all my friends will sit and eat with me in my Father's Kingdom." By this, I knew He anticipated what Stevenson calls "the completion of the universal Church and the marriage of the Lamb." I was honored to be the owner of the house.

And, you know, Jesus kept that promise. When I died a martyr, I entered my heavenly upper room, which was large, furnished, ready and waiting for me.

One will be ready for you, too. Will you make room for Jesus and become His follower? If so, let this poem by William A. Dunkerley help you:

> 'Mid all the traffic of the ways,
> Turmoils without, within,
> Make in my heart a quiet place,
> And come and dwell therein.
>
> A little shrine of quietness,
> All sacred to Thyself,
> Where Thou shalt all my soul possess,
> And I may find myself.
>
> A little shelter from life's stress,
> Where I may lay me prone,
> And bare my soul in loneliness,
> And know as I am known.
>
> A little place of mystic grace,
> Of self and sin swept bare,
> Where I may look upon Thy face,
> And talk with Thee in prayer.

9

John the Baptist

"Then Jesus came from Galilee to the Jordan to be baptized by John"
(Matthew 3:13)

I knew Jesus because He asked me to baptize Him.

I am John, the one who looks like a hippie from the 1970s, with long, uncombed hair, a scruffy beard, sandals and a coat made from camel skin. Make no wonder the people around Judea asked, "What then is this child going to be?" (John 1:66).

I spent most of my time fasting, praying, preaching and fending off wild beasts in the rugged desert around the Dead Sea. My diet was locusts and wild honey, but my spiritual food was God's holy law.

However, my outward appearance was misleading. It didn't match my heart, which was to do God's will and provoke others to do the same. Because of that, Jesus announced, "I tell you the truth: Among those born of women there has not risen anyone greater than John the Baptist" (Matthew 11:11).

I was born to the high priest, Zechariah, and his wife, Elizabeth, a couple too old to have children. But, God intervened, and I was born six months before Jesus.

Undoubtedly, that was according to God's plan. For, as Elijah was a forerunner of the nation of Israel, I was to be a forerunner, preparing the way for Jesus (Luke 1:76). Eventually, where the Jordan River flows into the Dead Sea, I preached repentance of sin and water baptism, immersing many Gentiles who wanted to become the people of God. People thought I was their Messiah, but I said, "I baptize you with water. But one more powerful than I will come, the thongs of whose sandals I am not worthy to untie. He will baptize you with the Holy Spirit and with fire" (Luke 3:16).

Then, the unexpected happened: Jesus asked *me* to baptize *Him*! However, I objected, saying, "I need to be baptized by you." But, Jesus insisted. "Let it be so now;" he said, "it is proper for us to do this to fulfill all righteousness." I agreed. When Jesus emerged from the water, I saw God's Spirit, descending like a dove on Him. God the Father declared, "This is my Son, whom I love; with him I am well pleased" (Matthew 3:14-15, 17).

When I baptized Jesus, I knew He had no sins to confess. He was simply identifying Himself with humanity. He did not want to appear as an untouchable.

As I said, Jesus' request for baptism was "to fulfill all righteousness." In other words, He would comply with all ordinances required for His ministry as Prophet, Priest and King. So, in order to be the High Priest over the House of God, He would observe each ordinance in the law of Moses.

Following His baptism, the Spirit directed Jesus into the desert, to be tempted by Satan (Mark 1:12-13). The day after the temptation, I proclaimed Him to be the Sacrificial Lamb, provided by God, to deal with humanity's sin.

What did I mean? I meant that Jesus was the Lamb of History (Genesis 22:8), the Passover Lamb (Exodus 12:2), and the Lamb of Prophecy (Isaiah 53:7). To erase the sin of the world, He would take humanity's place in death, as the ram died in Isaac's place (Genesis 22:13). Marcus L. Loane writes: "This would be the ultimate atonement for the sin of the world, and in a form that would fulfill all the demands of Hebrew ritual or ancient prophecy."

In my role as forerunner, I saw Jesus as the One designated by God the Father to deal with the sin problem. I knew Jesus was manifested to be the universal provision for sin in its root and fruit. He would take away the sin of the world, for both Jew and Gentile. As Isaiah said, it would be for "my people" (Isaiah 53:8) and, as Simeon predicted, it would be "a light for revelation to the Gentiles" (Luke 2:32). Later, the Apostle John confirmed it by declaring, "For God so loved the world" (John 3:16). That was the final announcement to point people away from me, the herald, and to focus on Jesus, the King.

Declaring Jesus to be the Lamb of God was the highlight of my ministry. And, since our ministries overlapped and my work as forerunner was ending, I wanted my disciples to follow Him. Herod violated Scripture by taking the wife of his brother, Philip (Leviticus 18:16). When I boldly rebuked him, he threw me into prison (Matthew 14:3-4). That's when the light of my ministry faded, and Jesus, "the light of the world" (John 8:12), shone in greater glory.

Eventually, Herod beheaded me (Matthew 14:10), but human violence could not subdue God's Kingdom. In fact, Jesus declared: "From the days of John the Baptist until now, the kingdom of heaven has been forcefully advancing, and forceful men lay hold of it" (Matthew 11:12). As John MacArthur writes, "[t]he kingdom presses ahead relentlessly, and only the relentless press their way into it."

Around that time, a conflict about baptism developed between some of my disciples and the Jews. Perhaps it was a certain Jew who was against Jesus. The question to me was, "Since the One I baptized is now baptizing, what was the spiritual value of my baptismal ministry?" My disciples were still loyal to me. In fact, to them, as Loane writes, "it seemed monstrous that one who owed so much to John's testimony should presume to intrude upon his field of work…. They would like to have thought that the ministry of baptism was John's prerogative, but they saw that John was surpassed by what Jesus was now doing."

However, I was undisturbed by this. Indeed, Jesus was supposed to grow greater, and I, less. So, it was proper that all come to Him. After all, "A man can receive only what is given him from heaven" (John 3:27). I was great, but Jesus was greater because, again as Loane writes, "God is the One unique source of truth and authority; man has no share in them at all unless he has received them as a gift which comes as it were from heaven." So, the fact that all came to Jesus was "proof that He was the One that had come down from heaven."

As Jesus' forerunner, I was the friend of the groom. That is, I acted on His behalf in winning the bride for Him and preparing for the wedding. The bride was greater than me. She belonged to the groom, whereas I was His friend.

About halfway through Jesus' ministry, from my prison cell, I sent a delegation to Him, asking, "Are you the one who was to come, or should we expect someone else?" (Matthew 11:3). My morale was low at the time, and Jesus' ministry was not following my plan. That is, instead of condemning sinners, He was forgiving them and healing the sick. How could He be the Messiah?

Jesus' candid answer was reliable: "Go back and report to John what you have seen and heard: The blind receive sight, the lame walk, those who have leprosy are cured, the deaf hear, the dead are raised, and the good news is preached to the poor. Blessed is the man who does not fall away on account of me" (Luke 7:22-23).

By His answer, I understood that, in Ron Rhodes' words, "these were the precise miracles prophesied to be performed by the Messiah when He came." Then, He turned to the crowd and declared, "I tell you the truth: Among those born of women there has not risen anyone greater than John the Baptist; yet he who is least in the kingdom of heaven is greater than he" (Matthew 11:11).

Admittedly, Jesus was much mightier than I. Henry Ward Beecher asks, "Why should we study acorns when we have oak trees among us?" I was the acorn; Jesus, the oak tree.

Although I was not Jesus' disciple, I was among those who actually touched Him. But, I was one of a few who believed Him to be God's Son. So, why did Jesus say there was none greater than me? Perhaps because I bridged the gap between the Old and New testaments. But, mainly, it was because of my self-effacement. While I was a successful prophet, I did not want the glory. Nor did I resent being replaced by Jesus. All I wanted was for people to meet and know Him.

When Jesus said that no mother's son was greater than me, I took it as a compliment. But, then He added, "he who is least in the kingdom of heaven is greater than he." What did He mean? Had I fallen short of the Kingdom of Heaven?

In my ministry, I laid the axe to the root of the trees, burning those which did not produce fruit. And, I assumed Jesus would do the same. In fact, when I announced Jesus' ministry, I prophesied, "I baptize you with water for repentance. But after me will come one who is more powerful than I, whose sandals I am not fit to carry. He will baptize you with the Holy Spirit and with fire. His winnowing fork is in his hand, and he will clear his threshing floor, gathering his wheat into the barn and burning up the chaff with unquenchable fire" (Matthew 3:11-12). However, to my surprise, Jesus invited to His kingdom the weak ones I had excluded. In that way, the least in the Kingdom were greater than me. Consequently, because Jesus didn't fit my pattern, I doubted He was the Messiah. Obviously, because He didn't fit my mold meant He was the One to come, the Messiah. I expected Him to ignore the "weak" and the "least," but He wanted to reach, cleanse and heal them.

Over the years, people have wondered what made me so popular. Jesus asked the multitudes that same question, "What did you go out into the desert to see? A reed swayed by the wind?" (Matthew 11:7). Obviously, the people were amazed with me, although all I wanted was for them to acknowledge their sin and repent. And, Jesus understood that. So, He explained that I was as common as a marsh reed, and just as weak, quoting Isaiah, "A bruised reed he will not break" (Isaiah 42:3). Jesus knew, in Loane's words, that "[m]en would not go and stand in the desert to see someone who bowed at the breath of the wind."

Jesus then asked, "[W]hat did you go to see? A man dressed in fine clothes?" (Matthew 11:8). He explained that men who wear fine clothes are not desert-goers. I was not their type. I was rough and ready, without any pursuit for personal luxury.

Jesus' third question was, "Then what did you go out to see? A prophet?" (Matthew 11:8). People were usually attracted to prophets. They believed I was a prophet (Matthew 21:26). I predicted and witnessed the coming of Jesus. In fact, His coming brought my ministry to an end.

Out of respect for Jesus, my disciples told Him of my death and burial. Obviously, He was disturbed, not only because we were cousins and partners in ministry, but because my martyrdom reminded Him of His own impending death. Understandably, He had to retire to the desert for rest and privacy (Matthew 14:12-13). After that, my disciples felt free to follow Him.

10

Judas Iscariot

"Then Judas Iscariot, one of the Twelve, went to
the chief priests to betray Jesus to them"
(Mark 14:10)

I knew Jesus because I betrayed Him with a kiss.
My name is Judas Iscariot, a Judean from South Palestine. I volunteered
to be Jesus' disciple, but He did not call me to be an apostle. I was the only
disciple from Judea. The remaining eleven were from Galilee.

As you know, Judas means "praise of God," and Iscariot means "son
of Kerioth," a village south of Jerusalem. Harry Rimmer writes that my
name "has become a byword in all civilized nations" and I have "become
an object of abhorrence."

Why have people reacted negatively to my name? Why hasn't my name
generated the respect of Peter and Paul, or Mary and Martha? Why haven't
mothers named their sons after me?

It's because the name "Judas Iscariot" has been stained with treachery,
and people hate traitors! In fact, most people would like to blot my name
from the pages of history. But, where does that leave those who call
themselves "Christian"? I can see them hating treachery, but aren't they
supposed to love traitors? I know I did wrong by betraying my Lord, but
I am human, in need of love, fairness and understanding.

Prophetically, David wrote about me: "Even my close friend, whom I trusted, he who shared my bread, has lifted up his heel against me" (Psalm 41:9). And, "May his days be few; may another take his place of leadership" (Psalm 109:8).

At the disciples' last meal with Jesus, Satan controlled my heart, driving me to do what I had to do. I led the officials to the Garden and, like a snake creeping through the grass, I approached Jesus and identified Him with a kiss. I turned against Him. And, as Friedrich August Tholuck writes, I betrayed "the Man without fault, without sin, the Man through whom…humanity rises to its true and proper dignity."

Remarkably, Jesus knew me and was prepared for my treachery. He was never deceived. But, why did I betray Him?

Well, even though Jesus knew who would betray Him, He never preordained me to do it. In fact, in spite of what He knew, He added me to His inner circle of disciples. Then, it became my choice to betray Him and seal my own destiny.

At the same time, being a member of the twelve disciples gave me the opportunity to seek a noble life. I was in a position to be good and do good, but I blew it. So, what attracted me to Jesus?

My first attraction was worldly ambition. I wanted to be part of Jewish independence and not be under Rome's oppression. And, I figured Jesus would help secure our freedom. After all, He was popular and fearless. But, His mission did not include earthly power, glory and honor.

Being a Judean, I was a true Jew, loyal to my nation and looking for our Messiah. I knew that when He appeared, our Jewish nation would triumph, and the Roman emperor would have to kneel at His feet. That thought alone so intrigued me that I eagerly embraced Jesus' invitation to join His band of twelve.

However, I had an ulterior motive, a secular ambition. I was double-minded. Attracted to a Messianic Jesus, I was pulled by the prospect of personal advantage. I had what you people call the "Judas syndrome." That is, I made friends with Jesus' enemies for my own benefit and profit. Little did I know it would back-fire.

My second and fatal attraction was my economic ego. Because I was Judean, it was understood we had the edge over Galileans. My gift was finances. To me, in Rimmer's words, "There is no gift possessed by man that cannot be used to the glory of God, if it is consecrated to His purposes." So, I could see myself being the treasurer of Jesus' little company. And, eventually, when He became King of the world, I would be His Minister of Finance. So, what attracted me to Jesus? Money. Not how much I could give, but how much I could get, regardless of how I got it.

By now, you are beginning to see the cords I was weaving to tie my plan together. First, I was disillusioned over Jesus' refusal to be king. Second, I was disappointed with His spiritual ideals over my materialistic ideals. Third, I was greedy for money. And fourth, I was disrespectful of others.

However, the more I twisted my diabolical braid, the weaker I became spiritually. As my greed developed, so did my self-justification. And, finances, my greatest ability, became my idol and the test of my character. In fact, it seemed like it had a noose around my neck, leading me to rob the treasury of Jesus' little band of disciples. And, I'm sure you agree that greed is what Rimmer calls the "root of almost every crime of violence that plagues the earth today."

Some of you may wonder why Jesus didn't expose and rebuke me. I don't know. But, I have seen His mercy, grace and patience many times. I agree with Isaiah who said, "A bruised reed he will not break, and a smoldering wick he will not snuff out" (Isaiah 42:3).

At this point, let me warn you about the love of money. It is not how much or how little you have, but how it controls you. Do you sin to get it? Do you cheat at tax time? And, do you step on others to get it?

These are questions I should have asked myself early in life. The fact is, as I learned, one of life's tragedies is to have godly principles, but not live by them. As a result, since I did not live as I pretended to believe, I soon began to believe as I lived. I persuaded myself that Christian imperatives were not an obligation. Eventually, Jesus' ethical standards meant practically nothing to me. To quote Rimmer, the greatest tragedy of sin is that "it gathers momentum until it is irresistible."

The question was, "What can I do to escape my dilemma?" I could become friends with Jesus' enemies and make it profitable for me. So, I went to the high priests and offered to betray Jesus for thirty pieces of silver (Matthew 26:15; Exodus 21:32). Actually, I was not only betraying Jesus' love and confidence, I was also using the majesty of Christ in a money-making scheme. Christ's holiness meant nothing to me.

That point was my lowest deed ever. But, it got worse. To carry out my scheme, I had to stay close to Jesus and His disciples. So, I went to the Upper Room and ate the Passover meal with them. You could have cut the tension with a knife. While we all sat around the table, Jesus said, "I tell you the truth, one of you is going to betray me" (John 13:21). John, who was sitting next to Jesus, asked, "Lord, who is it?" While we searched each other's faces, Jesus answered, "It is the one to whom I will give this piece of bread when I have dipped it in the dish" (John 13:26). So, He dipped the bread in some sauce and proceeded to pass it to the one disciple He wanted to honor. He handed the "sop" or moist bread to me!

As I took the bread, Satan controlled my every move, causing me to harden my perversity into determined wickedness. Jesus knew it and replied, "What you are about to do, do quickly" (John 13:27). So, I left the table, descended the steps, and crossed the courtyard to the narrow street. For the first time in my life, I was alone in the blackest night since Creation.

Around midnight, I led a haphazard mob of citizens, soldiers, Pharisees and chief priests to the Garden of Gethsemane. I knew Jesus would be there with His disciples, and I would be interrupting devotions. But I was out for revenge. On top of that, I was profaning the Passover, which James M. Stalker calls "the most sacred season of the entire year."

Stealing our way through the darkness, the mob carried clubs, lanterns and swords. Acting on orders from the high priests, we were to capture Jesus and bring Him to Annas, a Jewish high priest. But, the mob didn't know Jesus. Isn't it strange that, in Fulton J. Sheen's words, "those who are bent on evil cannot recognize Divinity even when it stands before them"?

In the event this would happen, I had agreed to identify Jesus. There, in the shadows, beneath the murky glare of the lanterns, I faced Jesus, greeted Him with "Greetings, Rabbi" and kissed Him (Matthew 26:49).

That was the sign of recognition for the soldiers. Mind you, being a man myself, I simply did not betray another man. I had betrayed the Son of Man (Daniel 7:13). I had planned it. And, according to Klass Schilder, it was a deliberate, "hearty kiss, but not a repeated kiss."

I don't know what I expected, but, to my surprise, Jesus asked, "Judas, are you betraying the Son of man with a kiss?" (Luke 22:49). He added, "Friend, do what you came for" (Matthew 26:50). Imagine, He called me His "friend," His "comrade." Even at my worst, He did not denounce me.

It seems strange to me now that I was known as Jesus' friend and "one of the twelve." Schilder comments, "Not one of the strangers, not one of the acquaintances, but one of the twelve, one of the specially gleaned group of intimate friends, delivered Jesus up into the hands of those who carried swords…."

I lost no time claiming the thirty pieces of silver, the wages for my sin. That money gave me some satisfaction, but I was overwhelmed with a new insight. I saw Jesus' love and I saw myself.

I was confused. Chrysostom, one of your church fathers, describes my condition like this: "The cleverness of the Devil consists in preventing man from suspecting the gravity of the sin before it is definitely committed, lest repentance should turn him away from it; but once the fault is committed, he allows the guilty one to feel its full gravity, in order to drive him to despair."

When Jesus was condemned to die, I was filled with remorse. So, with hurried step, I made my way back to the high priests. "I have sinned," I confessed, "for I have betrayed innocent blood." But, they were so busy gloating over their condemned prisoner, they proudly responded, "What is that to us? That's your responsibility" (Matthew 27:4). Realizing their callousness and nursing my guilt, in a mad rage, I flung the thirty pieces of blood money into the Temple and headed out into the unknown.

One of your authors, Hester H. Cholmondeley, has captured it well:

Still as of old
Men by themselves are priced —
For thirty pieces Judas sold
Himself, not Christ.

What does a man do with all he's seen and heard? I saw Jesus' wonderful miracles. I experienced His extreme goodness. I heard His marvelous words. Yet, I was empty and unmoved. A man should go back and start over, if he can.

Where does a man go when he has betrayed his Lord? Where does he go for love, fairness and understanding? As Isaac Watts writes:

> *What shall the dying sinner do*
> *That seeks relief for all his woe?*
> *Where shall the guilty conscience find*
> *Ease for torment of the mind?*

I ran into the streets and through the city gate. I had lived so close to Jesus. I had every opportunity for spiritual growth. I could have been forever wrapped with His arms of love. Instead, I went my own self-chosen way, fashioned my own noose, picked my own tree, and swung to my own place—into outer darkness!

11
Barabbas

"But the chief priests and the elders persuaded the crowd
to ask for Barabbas and to have Jesus executed"
(Matthew 27:20)

I knew Jesus because He took my place on the Cross.

My story took place on Good Friday. And, as it turned out, it was good for me. Leonard Griffith writes, "For nearly everyone else it turned out to be a bad, black and horrible day—for Jesus who died on the cross, for the two thieves who were crucified with him, for Judas who committed suicide, for the disciples who lost their dearest friend, Pilate who lost his self-respect, the soldiers who crucified an innocent man, the crowds who ran home beating their breasts." For them, it was a bad Friday. But, for me, it was good because I was released from prison.

My name is Barabbas. I was a Jewish zealot, a rebel who resisted the power of Rome. In fact, in Jerusalem, I was involved in an uprising, which included murder and other criminal activities. Ironically, I became the people's hero, exactly what they wanted, to help deliver them from the Romans. However, I was sent to prison to await my deserved execution.

As a zealot of Judea, I, along with my followers, belonged to a group of fanatical Jews. We were freedom fighters, whose aim it was to rid the country of the Romans. Our own Jewish historian, Flavius Josephus, reports that zealots "had daggers under their garments."

The Belgian dramatist, Michel de Ghelderode, describes me like this: "He is a tough, unrepentant ruffian who boasts of his murderous exploits and declares proudly that it took a whole battalion of soldiers to arrest him and bring him to justice. A priest comes to the door of the dungeon and whispers that things may not turn out as badly as he expects."

To maintain custom, the Roman governor, Pontius Pilate, was expected to pardon one prisoner each year at Passover. And, since he found no fault in Jesus of Nazareth, Pilate assumed He should be set free. But, the Jews, desiring the pardon of a prisoner, demanded the death of Jesus of Nazareth. So, Pilate agreed.

Tradition has it that my real name is Jesus Barabbas, a descendant of Cain. The name "Barabbas" means "son of a father," most likely a rabbi. I was also a student of the scribes. However, being a thief and a murderer made me similar to Jesus of Nazareth, who was accused of the same crimes. So, when Pilate asked, "What shall I do, then, with Jesus who is called Christ?" (Matthew 27:22), he was separating one Jesus from the other, me from Christ. In fact, an early church scholar, Origen, dropped the name "Jesus" from my name, because he didn't want the real Jesus associated with a criminal. After all, to him, Jesus, the Christ, was the Son of God!

The truth is that Pilate wanted to save Jesus, the Christ. So, he offered the people a choice—Christ or me. Pilate was convinced they would choose Christ. "But the chief priests stirred up the crowd to have Pilate release [me] instead" (Mark 15:11).

I was surprised when the people yelled, "Barabbas!" I remember it well. I was sitting in my gloomy cell, staring at my hands, which the Romans would soon pierce with spikes. Imagining the hammering, I shuddered at my impending crucifixion. Suddenly, I heard the crowd outside, roaring in unison. Like a Greek chorus, their hoarse throats shouted violently, "Crucify him! Crucify him! Release Barabbas!" I am positive I heard my own name.

Then, I heard heavy steps. Following the priest, the jail guard approached my filthy dungeon cell, unlocked the door, and removed the chains from my hands and feet. "Barabbas," he said, "you're free. The crowd has called for your release. Jesus, the Christ, is taking your place." But, I had done nothing to deserve a pardon.

"Who? What? Why me?" I asked, stunned. But the guard ordered me to join the procession on its way to Calvary. There, the Place of a Skull, I heard the hammer-blows, nailing the Christ to a rough wooden cross. I saw the Roman soldiers raise the Cross towards the clouds. Then, the Christ called out, "Father, forgive them, for they do not know what they are doing" (Luke 23:34). A centurion exclaimed, "Surely this man was the Son of God!" (Mark 15:39).

Standing in awe, I could hardly believe my eyes. My heart raced. (I do have a heart, you know.) I felt for that innocent man. He took my place. He was my substitute. I was the murderer. I should have been on that cross. I deserved hell. But, that man did nothing wrong. Governor Pilate could find no fault in Him. Pilate's wife said He was an "innocent man" (Matthew 27:19). Your great Apostle Paul wrote that "God made him who had no sin to be sin for us, so that in him we might become the righteousness of God" (2 Corinthians 5:21).

But, why me? Why not one of the robbers who were crucified with Jesus, the Christ? I guess I will never know.

To that point, Jesus had been quite popular. So, why did the crowd want Him crucified? From what I put together, the Jewish religious authorities dominated the crowd, with their henchmen scattered throughout the courtyard. They figured that, while Jesus was a rebel, He was more interested in spiritual things than politics. In fact, He claimed to be God, even forgiving people's sins. Besides, His followers were hiding, out of fear of arrest. And, because Jesus was arrested late at night, most of His followers did not know His whereabouts. Obviously, He was not going to lead them in any rebellion.

Again I ask, "Why me? Why was I set free, and Jesus, the Christ, bound and nailed to a cross?" Everyone knew I was a bandit and robber. I wonder, *Is that why the Jews have always been robbed and persecuted?*

I have another question, "Why did Pilate give in to the wishes of the crowd?" He had declared Jesus faultless. He was impressed with what Frederick W. Krummacher calls "Jesus' moral purity and innocence."

I know the answer now, as do the priests, scribes, Sadducees, Pharisees and Sanhedrin, for they all were in on the plot. The truth is, Pilate was a coward and a people-pleaser. He couldn't handle conflict. He would rather excuse himself and walk away.

For Jesus, the Christ, it must have been perplexing. Not that He doubted His Father's will, but that those against Him were citizens of Jerusalem. They had heard His words, seen His miracles, and felt His love.

Looking back at it now, I agree with Klass Schilder that "[t]he masses are agreeing with the intent of the Sanhedrin. 'They all say unto Pilate: Let him be crucified.' All is an inclusive word. It refers to the chief priests not only, but to the people also; not only to the Pharisees, but also to the man in the street. Not only to the vengeful enemies, but also to the timid spectators. The fire of hell spreads over the whole crowd, and a mad cry vibrates over the square: *He* must be sent to the cross."

John Newton's hymn, "I Saw One Hanging on a Tree," expresses it well:

> *My conscience felt and owned the guilt,*
> *And plunged me in despair,*
> *I saw my sins His blood had spilt,*
> *And helped to nail Him there.*

As I understand it, that means "substitution." That's what Jesus, the Christ, did for me. He acted on my behalf. He took my place. He gave His life, so mine could be spared. Mark, the writer of your second Gospel, says Christ "gave his life as a ransom for many" (Mark 10:45).

Again, according to your Bible, our father Abraham knew what "substitute" meant. When he was about to sacrifice his son, Isaac, God provided a ram instead (Genesis 22:1-14). In the same way, Jesus, the Christ, gave Himself for me. And, because I represent all people, He did that for you, too; or as F.E. Marsh puts it, "the Holy for the unholy; the Sinless for the sinful; the Immortal for the mortal; for what but His righteousness could cover our sins? O sweet changes! O unsearchable work! O unexampled benefit, that the wickedness of many should be covered by the One righteous, the righteousness of One should justify many sinners!"

And all that reminds me of Ellis J. Crum's chorus:

> *He paid a debt He did not owe;*
> *I owed a debt I could not pay;*
> *I needed someone to wash my sins away.*
> *And, now, I sing a brand new song, "Amazing Grace."*
> *Christ Jesus paid a debt that I could never pay.*

In my rebel days, I hurt, even killed, people, whether they deserved it or not. I substituted for no one. But, Jesus, the Christ, became my substitute, took my punishment, died in my place, and paid for my sin. It's like the words of a hymn, written by William G. Ovens and Gladys W. Roberts:

> *Wounded for me, wounded for me,*
> *There on the cross He was wounded for me;*
> *Gone my transgressions, and now I am free,*
> *All because Jesus was wounded for me.*
>
> *Dying for me, dying for me,*
> *There on the cross He was dying for me;*
> *Now in His death my redemption I see,*
> *All because Jesus was dying for me.*

To me, that was the great exchange—His righteousness for my wretchedness, His death for my life, and His salvation for my sin. Simply put, again as Marsh writes, "Substitution is for the believing sinner, for Christ has borne his sin and he will not have to bear it."

An old hymn by Philip P. Bliss explains it well:

> *Bearing shame and scoffing rude,*
> *In my place condemned He stood;*

Sealed my pardon with His blood.
Hallelujah! What a Savior!

John says that, when Jesus, the Christ, willingly went to the Cross, he "lay down [his] life for the sheep" (John 10:15). Paul says He "died for us" (Romans 5:8), was made "a curse for us" (Galatians 3:13), and died "the righteous for the unrighteous" (1 Peter 3:18). To me, He provided protection, like a mother hen covers her chicks at her own expense.

That was a good example of substitution. Emil Brunner explains: "In the cross of Christ God says to man: There is where you ought to be. Jesus, my Son, hangs there in your stead. You are the rebel who should be hanged on the gallows. But lo, I suffer instead of you and because of you, because I love you in spite of what you are. My love for you is so great that I meet you there with My love, there on the cross. I cannot meet you anywhere else. You must meet me there by identifying yourself with the One on the cross. It is by this identification that I, God, can meet you, man, in him, saying to you what I say to him, 'My beloved Son.' "

With all this in mind, I can relate totally to "Eve's Lamentation," from the early Irish:

I am Eve, great Adam's wife,
'Twas my guilt took Jesus' life.
Since of Heaven I robbed my race,
On His Cross was my true place.

When Jesus, the Christ, died for the ungodly, the unjust, the lawless and the unrighteous, He died for me. That means He died, in the words of Charles Hodge, for all "sinners, for those who deserve wrath instead of love…those who were at once corrupt and the enemies of God."

As a former lawbreaker myself, I understand Peter saying that Christ died "the righteous for the unrighteous." As William Barclay states, that's quite "extraordinary…. It looks like injustice…. The suffering of Christ was for us; and the mystery is that he who deserved no suffering bore that suffering for us who deserved to suffer. He sacrificed himself to restore our lost relationship with God."

Now that it is all over, I must confess I admired Jesus, the Christ. He impressed me, moving me to see Him as my Substitute. I could not refuse His sacrifice. I would become His follower. In fact, if I had known it then, I would have quoted Shakespeare's words about Brutus:

> *His life was gentle, and the elements*
> *So mix'd in him,*
> *That Nature might stand up*
> *And say to all the world, "This was a man!"*

12
Simon of Cyrene

*"A certain man from Cyrene, Simon,…was passing by on his way
in from the country, and they forced him to carry the cross"*
(Mark 15:21)

I knew Jesus because I carried His cross.

My name is Simon, or Niger (Acts 13:1). I am a Hellenistic, Greek-speaking Jew from Cyrene, a Roman province in Northern Africa. Some say I was a pagan black man.

On the day of Jesus' crucifixion, things looked normal, but hopeful, for me. John Calvin Reid says, "The birds were singing, the sun was shining, God was in His heaven, all was right with the world—then suddenly everything changed."

At noon, dark clouds hid the sun. The earth shook, splitting rocks and mountains. Graves reopened and bodies came to life and walked in Jerusalem. And, in the Temple, the heavy curtain ripped from top to bottom!

In the first century, Cyrene was close to where Bengazi is today. I had a wife and two sons. We were devout worshipers of the one true God. Because of this, we traveled more than 1,000 miles to the Passover Festival of Unleavened Bread in our temple at Jerusalem. And, we would stay the fifty-some days afterwards for the Feast of Pentecost. In fact, our Law said all Jewish males were to go to our holy city three times a year for the feasts of Booths, Passover and Pentecost.

This is how I met Jesus. I did not believe He was the Christ, the anointed Messiah of Jehovah. But, on that eventful day, I was forced to change my direction. That's what your Bible calls "conversion" and "repentance." I was compelled to cancel my own plans and go His way. I was conscripted to carry His cross!

I remember it well. We had sailed for about two weeks and arrived safely at the port of Joppa. From there, we walked for two days, until we crested a hill and saw the City of David in the distance.

Since we were not wealthy, we had to stay outside the city. So, we camped near the west wall and went into the city for the celebrations on the various days for reading our Scriptures in the different synagogues. Ours was the Synagogue of Cyrene.

After about a week, on Friday evening, the beginning of Passover, the people of our synagogue (Acts 6:9), all Cyrenian Jews, headed towards the city to prepare our Passover lamb. Just before reaching the gate, we experienced the climax of our entire trip. We met a noisy crowd on their way to Jerusalem. Three condemned men, each carrying his own heavy cross, led the throng. A band of Roman soldiers pushed and hassled prisoners through the busy streets in order to intimidate the people. Two of the three were dirty, profane and murderous.

However, the third appeared kind, noble and patient, but looked as though he had been physically abused. Reid says, "A crown of thorns encircled His brow. Caked streaks of blood stained His pale, unshaven cheeks; the back of His robe was ghastly red. His hands trembled as they clutched His cross, and as He came opposite me He staggered and stumbled." He looked so weak. He had lost so much blood! The crowd jostled and shouted, "Crucify him! Crucify him!" (Luke 23:21). It appeared as though He would fall. I instinctively reached out to help Him, even to keep the Cross from dragging on the ground.

I wondered, *Doesn't He have any family or friends? Or, is He a stranger in Palestine?* I later learned He had friends. But, where were they? I was told He had healed hundreds, but they were conspicuous by their absence.

I found out He had twelve followers, but they all forsook Him and fled. He didn't have anybody to help Him carry His cross. Then, a Roman soldier grabbed my shoulder and commanded me to carry it. It was useless for me to object.

At that moment, I wanted to lose myself in the crowd. Instead, I was lifting a heavy cross and heading towards Calvary, the Place of a Skull!

It's all history now, but no other man ever saw such a procession of death or carried the actual wooden cross of Jesus.

My personal plans changed in a second and my life altered forever. I was something like Joseph. One minute, he was visiting his brothers in Dothan (Genesis 37:17), the next, he was thrown into a well (Genesis 37:24). Then, he was sold as a slave to traveling merchants (Genesis 37:28). Finally, he was falsely accused and thrown in prison. Life has its twists and turns.

One of your generation's writers, Leslie D. Weatherhead, tells of a rich young farmer who was converted and called into the ministry. At once, he sold his house, lands and life-stock, and prepared to go to Bible college. However, on his way, a bad accident left him with a broken back. By the time he was discharged from hospital, he was penniless and a cripple. All his dreams and plans ended in tragedy and disappointment. Although he kept his faith in God, his whole life lay at his feet in ashes.

The irony is, I was from Cyrene, not Jerusalem. I was a foreigner. That must have really humiliated Christ. He was the powerful King of the Jews, and yet I, a Greek-speaking Jew, had to carry His cross. He was making Himself nothing and adopting "the very nature of a servant" (Philippians 2:7). By taking His cross, I associated Him with nobodies.

So, you can see why I resented being conscripted like that. Why should this Roman soldier, this self-elected lord, treat people like cattle? Why was he picking on us Jews from Africa? I resented Him and that cross, that Roman instrument of death, as I resented the hangman's noose.

You see, the Romans had a terrible law. They could ask you to carry anything for one mile. They call it the "law of conscription." In this case, when someone was about to be crucified, no one would even touch a cross, let alone carry it! If he did, he would be unclean. I especially rebelled because it was Passover time and I would be ceremonially unclean. Besides, the soldiers would laugh at me, and the passersby would associate me with the condemned.

So, I questioned the whole thing. Wouldn't the people get more fun out of seeing the criminal carrying his own cross? Why should I have to do it? Maybe the high priests thought it unwise for Jesus, a son of Abraham, to break a law by carrying a burden on a feast day. Or, perhaps Jesus had carried it far enough, to the city gate. Someone else should take it to Golgotha. Whatever the reason, I was compelled or pressed into service, and I objected to it. But, what could I do against Rome's military hand?

I could do nothing. I was helpless and insulted. At the same time, it was a privilege to be associated with Christ. I was honored to represent suffering Christians faithfully following their Leader. Years later, people said I represented the long-anticipated re-gathering of Israel (Isaiah 43:5-7; 54:1-3).

But, why me? Some say I was nearest to the condemned One. Others suggest I was known as a secret disciple. A few believe I had scolded the soldiers for how they treated Christ. The truth is, I was the only one who helped the Messiah in His time of need. It was more than sympathy; it was empathy. I cared.

Oh, the complexity of it all! I was angry and bitter, yet, I was blessed and honored. I was shamed and humiliated, picked on and used. Yet, to the end of my days, I will always stand up for that God-Man. He won my heart! Like your Apostle Paul, I declare, "May I never boast except in the cross of our Lord Jesus Christ" (Galatians 6:14).

We finally reached the place of crucifixion, the hill shaped like a skull. The soldiers took the Cross from my shoulders and hurled it to the ground. Then, they manhandled Christ and stretched Him upon it. First, they hammered spikes in His hands and feet. They raised the Cross, with its victim, and dropped it into a hole. Your Scripture says they "crucified him." Then, four soldiers at each cross sat down and watched Him (Matthew 27:35-36).

I can't believe it. To think I carried His cross to this! It seems like a dream. But, I witnessed the whole thing. I saw the soldiers offer Him wine and vinegar. I read the title over His head, "This is Jesus, the King of the Jews" (Matthew 27:37). I witnessed them casting lots for His seamless robe.

I heard them, too. I heard the scribes and chief priests mocking and daring Him to come down from the Cross. I heard Christ asking God, His Father, why He had forsaken Him. And, I heard His last gasp for breath. Then, I heard the ripping of the heavy temple curtain from top to bottom, as if hit by a lightening rod! And, across the Kidron Valley, no doubt because he could see into the Holy of Holies, a soldier exclaimed, "Surely this man was the Son of God!" (Mark 15:39).

But, why? Why Him? Why was I conscripted by soldiers? Why was He forsaken by God, His Father? Why?

Well, His first three cries were for the needs of others. His last three were for His own needs. But, this middle cry had a deeper meaning. It happened while He poured Himself out in sacrificial death.

He looked like a worm. He was helpless in a circle of dogs and bulls smelling blood, snarling and gaping at Him. His bones were out of joint, His heart was as dry as wax, and His tongue stuck to His jaws. Finally, they tore off His clothes and left Him naked, hanging and dying in shame and utter disgrace. And, the crowd loved it, jeered Him, and looked for more. But, when His Father could watch it no longer, He drew a three-hour veil of darkness around the Cross to shield His only Son from what Marcus L. Loane calls "the eyes of a coarse and pitiless multitude."

I believe the darkness was merciful. It covered His nakedness and subdued the scorn. But suddenly, at the ninth hour, out of the mysterious darkness, Jesus gave a loud cry, "My God, why have you forsaken me?" (Matthew 27:46).

Why? Because He knew He was our Substitute. He knew His hour had come. So, He was not devastated at being forsaken. God cannot forsake God. Both Jesus and the Jews had repeated Psalm 22 numerous times. Now, He quoted it in fulfillment. In fact, God His Father was still with Him in His abandonment. God had heard His cry and accepted His sacrifice. Oh, the mystery of mercy!

Writing about me some years later, one of your anonymous poets said:

Simon of Cyrene bore
The cross of Jesus; nothing more,
His name is never heard again,
Nor honored by historic pen;
Not on the pedestal of fame
His image courts the loud acclaim
Simon of Cyrene bore.
The cross of Jesus; nothing more.

And yet, when all our work is done,
And golden beams the western sun
Upon a life of wealth and fame—
A thousand echoes ring the name—
Perhaps our hearts will humbly pray
"Good Master, let the record say,
Upon the page divine, 'He bore
The cross of Jesus,' nothing more."

Nothing more? Not really? For, what happened after Calvary became the turning point of history. Three days following His crucifixion, "There was a violent earthquake, for an angel of the Lord came...and...rolled back the stone" of the sepulcher (Matthew 28:2). The guards shook with fear and became as dead.

Then, the angel announced to the women, "I know that you are looking for Jesus, who was crucified. He is not here; he has risen, just as he said. Come and see the place where he lay" (Matthew 28:5-6).

And indeed, He was most assuredly alive. He appeared to Mary Magdalene and two travelers on the Emmaus road. Not only did Peter, Paul, James and the twelve disciples see Him, but so did over 500 others at one time (1 Corinthians 15:5-8). In fact, Luke records "he showed himself...and gave many convincing proofs that he was alive. He appeared to them over a period of forty days and spoke about the kingdom of God" (Acts 1:3).

Just think, because I carried His cross, my friends and I had ringside seats in this moving drama. We saw His crucifixion. We were in the area during His resurrection. And, we were there for the Feast of Pentecost. "When the day of Pentecost came…there were staying in Jerusalem God-fearing Jews from every nation under heaven." That included a group from "the parts of Libya near Cyrene." We were there to worship in our synagogue. We heard about the "sound like the blowing of a violent wind" and we "heard them speaking in his own language." In fact, they were "declaring the wonders of God in our own tongues!" (Acts 2:1, 5, 10, 2-3, 6, 8, 11).

My friends, my family and I will never forget that Passover and Festival. But, to think that, because of my rebellion, I could have missed it.

I don't suppose it's any different in your day. I imagine people still repel the Cross of Christ. For me, it took self-denial and sacrifice. And, that's the same challenge the risen Christ makes to you. In your own Scripture, He declares, "If anyone would come after me, he must deny himself and take up his cross and follow me" (Mark 8:34).

This has to be the great paradox of the Gospel. People, who once spurned the Cross, now carry it. People, who once defied Christ, now find delight in Him. People, who once denied Christ, now exclaim, "I am not ashamed of the gospel, because it is the power of God for the salvation of everyone who believes" (Romans 1:16).

But, why do so many turn away from His cross? You want His salvation, forgiveness and peace, but you refuse His invitation. Why? Why do you avoid His cross? For me, I was forced to carry it. But, you are not—you have a choice.

Do you know what it means to carry Christ's cross? It certainly is more than affliction, sorrow and the cares of this life. These are universal burdens, not crosses.

One of your writers, Clovis G. Chappell, tells of a beautiful and charming Southern girl. She was engaged to marry a young man of equal ability. But, death took her mother and brother within a week of each other. She was left with an invalid father and only brother. Consequently, this crushed her hopes for marriage. And, by the time spring had changed to fall, this fresh young girl had prematurely aged. Burdens not her own had wrecked her life.

For you in this twenty-first century, to bear Christ's cross involves voluntary sacrifice in either confessing or serving Him. It may include taking your stand for righteousness, and enduring ridicule and persecution. To bear the Cross means to deny yourself in order to win others to Christ. To bear the Cross means giving of your time, money, children, or your very life, in order to promote missions. Yes, cross-bearing always involves doing something for Christ at personal cost. And, as one of your French writers, Charles de Foucauld, puts it, "Crosses release us from this world and by doing so bind us to God."

Reid tells the following story.

"A well-known minister of your generation has illustrated the meaning of a cross-bearing by telling the story of Subrahmanyam, a young student in India who heard the call of Christ one night while attending a Methodist mission church in Madras. Subrahmanyam came from a Brahmin family, his father was the head of the Brahmin community. When he reported to his father what had happened, one might say that the whole village blazed up in anger. To try to make him change his mind, they tied him to a pillar in the courtyard of their house, stripped his turban from his head—which is itself a mark of indignity in the East—lashed his back with whips until the blood ran, and left him standing hour after hour through the burning noontide. They even had the contents of the sewage can poured over his head. To his grave he will carry two horrible scars, one on either cheek, where his tormentors burned his face with red hot irons, threatening to put out his eyes. When these men had done their worst and had gone off to the temple, Subrahmanyam's sister slipped out and cut his bonds and he escaped to the hills. In due time, he prepared himself for the Christian ministry and became one of the best known and most highly honored Methodist ministers in all India."

Let me ask you: what cross do you carry? What do you suffer in order to worship Christ and witness for Him? Are you ever tried for your faith, or do you live the way the world lives? Do you ever sacrifice your time and money? Do you think only of self? In other words, have you given up everything in order to take up Christ's cross?

Looking back, I was highly honored to carry His cross to Calvary. As Reid explains it, I feel I was blessed more than "Mary and Martha who gave Him lodging…the 'goodman of the house' who provided the upper room for the Last Supper…Joseph of Arimathea who gave Him a tomb… [and] Nicodemus who anointed His body for burial." Yes, I was doubly blessed. Not because I walked by His side or attended the Passover festival, but because I carried His cross and, in effect, His cross became mine. In fact, I was the first to learn that "anyone who does not carry [Jesus'] cross and follow [Him] cannot be [His] disciple" (Luke 14:27).

Carrying Christ's cross has its rewards. For one thing, as your Scriptures point out, it makes you His disciple (Luke 14:27), identifies you with Him and His sufferings (Galatians 2:30), and gives you new life (Luke 9:23-27).

And, what was my reward for carrying His cross that day? My reward was twofold.

First, I became His disciple. The fact that I was there, and the warm way He looked at me, convinced me. I would serve Him the rest of my life. Just as I had taken up His cross, so I would carry His cross. Just as I would carry His cross, so I would follow Christ all the way to Calvary and beyond. Indeed, when He said to the thief, "today you will be with me in paradise" (Luke 23:43), I felt He meant me, too.

My second reward concerned my two sons, Alexander and Rufus. They were dear to my heart. In fact, while I carried Christ's cross, I prayed they would follow my example. I was proud to be their father, now that I was following Christ. And, many nights after, I had quite the bedtime story for them. In time, they became leaders in the Christian Church, for Mark mentions them as my sons (Mark 15:21). Paul even says Rufus was "chosen in the Lord" (Romans 16:13).

To me, that's the greatest joy of any parent—to see their children serving Christ in His Church and the world. To you parents in these last days, let me encourage you to be an example to your children. Let them see you bearing the Cross. Let them feel your love. Let them hear your prayers. And, let them know you understand them. That will be your greatest joy—your most cherished memory!

Take it from me. I carried His cross!

13

The Nail-and-Hammer Man

"Here they crucified him, and with him two others—
one on each side and Jesus in the middle"
(John 19:18)

I knew Jesus because I nailed Him to His cross.

Your Holy Scriptures refer to a certain place, without identifying its whereabouts. It even tells of your God and Savior often secluding to "certain" unknown areas (Luke 5:22). And, it writes about a "certain" man, without giving his name (John 4:46).

Now, it's my turn.

I have a name, a Roman name, but it is unrecorded. Actually, I am a "certain" soldier, one of four, who helped to crucify Jesus of Nazareth. In fact, your fourth Gospel says, "Here they crucified him, and with him two others—one on each side and Jesus in the middle" (John 19:18). More than a "certain soldier," I preferred the title, "the Nail-and-Hammer Man."

On that dismal day, I had already nailed the hands and feet of two victims on crosses. So, my soldier buddies agreed that I should nail this one, as well. Interestingly, I discovered that innocent hands are different from guilty hands. But, as Calvin Miller writes, a "hammer man only drives the nails where the state says to drive them."

Miller also believes "it is mostly the guilty who crucify the innocent. The cross is but one more example of James Russell Lowell's 'truth forever on the scaffold, wrong forever on the throne.' "

On this point, Miller confesses, "This is where I see myself. I'm good with a hammer! Give me one and I'll nail you every chance I get. In fact, in three days I'll wreck the world! Like the official opposition, it's my nature to criticize, complain and accuse."

That was how we treated our "criminal." We had fun insulting and mocking Him. We knew how to "hammer" Him, even before we got to Golgotha, the Place of a Skull.

When we arrested Jesus, we bound and shackled Him as a prisoner. That was to humiliate Him. Second, we removed His clothes, dressed Him in a gorgeous purple robe, and pretended He was a king. Third, we tied Him to a public post and lashed Him senseless with the cat-o-nine tails. Fourth, we twisted a vine of thorns into a crown and pressed it on His head. Fifth, we placed a stick in His hand, mockingly bowed before Him, and spat in His face. Sixth, we blindfolded Him, to continue playing the "King-game." That is, we pushed Him around, took turns slapping Him, and then made Him guess who had struck Him. It was what you call "hazing."

Our Roman style of crucifixion—impaling someone on a cross—was a cruel way of punishing criminals. But, we were used to it. In fact, that was part of my job as a State employee. So, to me, all criminal hands and feet looked alike. That is, all except the hands and feet of this One. He was different.

We roughly grabbed Jesus and maneuvered Him under his heavy cross. Then, we pushed and shoved our way along the Via Dolorosa. But, the ordeal was too much for Him. So, we conscripted Simon to carry the cross behind Him. By the time we reached Calvary, Jesus was already a mess of dust, sweat and blood. His head was bleeding from His thorny crown. His back was red and blood-clotted from the thirty-nine lashes. And, what was left of His beard was full of spittle. So, He could not resist. He was putty in our hands. In fact, it seemed He submitted simply because He loved someone.

At that point, I became the center of attention. I knew I was being watched. I was extremely self-conscious, but, I liked being in control. I had a job to do, and I meant to do it well. In fact, as "the nail-and-hammer man," according to Miller, I made sure no one unfastened "the Master from the wood."

Most of the crowd stared in wide-eyed wonder and fear. Many women wept openly, constantly dabbing their eyes with their headdress. The disciples and the fishermen looked lost, like baby chicks searching for their mother.

On the other hand, the kings and governors were delighted. The prostitutes and tax collectors waited to see the outcome. Some laughed, while peasants, relatives and His followers wept and moaned, "My Lord! My Lord! My Lord!" As I asked myself, "Who is this man?," we stripped off His clothes, stretched Him over the rough wood, and spread His arms on the crossbeam.

He lay motionless, the picture of an abuse victim. Some women wanted to help, but they were afraid of the soldiers. As for me, I bravely stood erect, gripping my mallet-like hammer and three ten-inch nails. At my captain's command, I briskly straddled the criminal and positioned the first nail. Raising the hammer, I swung with towering force. *Smack! Crack!* I quickly placed the second nail. *Smack! Crack!* His hands stiffened and opened. Then, the third nail. *Smack! Crack!* His feet twisted and His whole body shivered. A few women screamed and ran from the hill. Men watched and waited. Eventually, I slowly arose and stepped aside, holding a Roman hammer covered with the Redeemer's blood.

As I understand it, His left hand represented sin, which could only be paid for by blood. So, hammering His left hand meant "cancelling the written code, with its regulations, that was against us and that stood opposed to us; he took it away, nailing it to the cross" (Colossians 2:14). He was wiping out the charge-list of our self-admitted debts.

What did this mean? It was the same as if we had signed a note, acknowledging our indebtedness. As Israel had failed to keep the written Law (Exodus 24:3), so we had failed to keep the unwritten law in our hearts (Romans 2:14-15). The nail in Christ's left hand represented His one sacrifice, to deal with the sin question.

I've also heard that Christ's right hand represented the holiness of God, which could only be satisfied by blood. And, Christ's feet represented Satan's defeat, the seed of the woman bruising his head. Little did I know the part I played in God's pardoning grace!

An eerie silence, like a wet blanket, fell over the hill. Mockers and scoffers tried to make sense of the deadly drama. But, most of the spectators on Mount Calvary had an expression of "What now?" Some didn't know what to think. Others couldn't think what to do. Miller depicts me with the blood of God "dripping from the steel head of a hammer."

My captain shattered the stillness with, "Let's get it done!" So, my three buddies and I manhandled cross and victim towards the sky, securing the post in a hole in the ground. Then, we sat and waited to see what might happen.

But, why wait when we could have even more fun? We decided to share Christ's clothing among us and gamble for His seamless robe. But, we didn't know we were actually fulfilling the prophecy, "They divide my garments among them and cast lots for my clothing" (Psalm 22:18). This is what Miller calls "one mysterious moment when history froze into focus the cross of Christ."

One of your poets, James Weldon Johnson, expresses it like this:

> *On Calvary, on Calvary,*
> *They crucified my Jesus.*
> *They nailed him to the cruel tree,*
> *And the hammer!*
> *The hammer!*
> *The hammer!*
> *Rang through Jerusalem's streets*
> *The hammer!*
> *The hammer!*
> *The hammer!*
> *Rang through Jerusalem's streets.*
> *Jesus, my lamb-like Jesus,*
> *Shivering as the nails go through his hands;*
> *Jesus, my lamb-like Jesus,*

Shivering as the nails go through his feet.
Jesus, my darling Jesus,
Groaning as the Roman spear plunged in his side;
Jesus, my darling Jesus,
Groaning as the blood came spurting from his wound.
Oh, look how they done my Jesus!

To me, the whole scene was one big paradox. I mean, Jesus' naked body sagging on the nails, yet over His head a plaque read, "This is Jesus, the King of the Jews" (Matthew 27:37). I didn't know what was right about it, but, for some strange reason, it seemed the whole thing was orchestrated to create something good for someone.

Then, there were the passersby, praising Him for building the Temple in three days, but pleading with Him that, if He were God's Son, to come down from the Cross.

Again, if such claims were true, then surely He was part of the bigger picture which, some say, is God's plan for the world's redemption.

If that wasn't enough, the scribes, robbers and chief priests mocked and insulted Him. They wanted a king, but they couldn't see Jehovah God having a Son to fill that role.

He hung there as a public spectacle. He could not turn or adjust Himself, to ease His pain. His hands were powerless to brush away the flies, shade His eyes or cover His shame. Nor could He close His ears to the jeering crowd. He was lifted and put on public display as one accursed, even before He died.

You have no way of knowing if I ever became one of His followers. So, what effect did all this have on me? I will admit that, when I heard Him struggle and say, "Father, forgive them, for they do not know what they are doing" (Luke 23:34), I knew He included me.

Soon afterwards, He promised a robber, "[T]oday you will be with me in paradise" (Luke 23:43). Imagine, a robber with broken legs, walking with Jesus in heaven!

By noon, halfway through Jesus' six hours on the Cross, darkness shrouded the hill for three hours. I had openly abused and violated His body. My hammer and nails had ripped His flesh apart. Undoubtedly, Jesus felt God the Father coming at Him from all sides—holiness, justice, sin and death.

Jesus was under what Klass Schilder calls the "catastrophic curse." Make no wonder He shouted, "Eloi, Eloi, lama sabachthani?... My God, my God, why have you forsaken me?" (Mark 15:34). Was He afraid of death on a Roman cross? No, but He feared losing fellowship and His close relationship with His Father. He then called, "I am thirsty" (John 19:28), and they gave Him vinegar.

I remember seeing Mary, His mother, sobbing near the Cross. He spoke to her kindly, "Dear woman, here is your son" and, to John, He said, "Here is your mother" (John 19:26-27).

And, with His work for our salvation completed, He announced, "It is finished" (John 19:30). He then committed His spirit into His Father's care and breathed His final breath. The Temple veil split from top to bottom and a centurion exclaimed, "Surely, this was a righteous man" (Luke 23:47).

Miller comments, "Once upon a tree, our Savior bled a royal river of access, whose rich blood ended in eternity. Drop by drop his war against sin drove back the forces of hell until every drop was gone. 'It is finished,' cried the Son, and the angels broke the universal hush with the battle cry of human liberation."

Since that eventful day, people have asked, "For whom did you do this?" Back then, I would have said, "For Rome." But, I like to think that, for some reason, I did it for others.

I made those nail-prints for Thomas. Years later, he saw them and confessed, "My Lord and my God!" (John 20:28).

I hammered those nails for Peter, who declared that "wicked men… put [Jesus] to death by nailing him to the cross" (Acts 2:23).

I created those nail-scars for Paul, who said, "[H]e took [the written code] away, nailing it to the cross" (Colossians 2:14).

Most of all, my nails and the centurion's spear bruised Jesus for the Jews, God's chosen people. Some day soon, "They will look on the one they have pierced" (John 19:37).

At the same time, I pounded those nails for the world's many hymn-writers! For example, Fanny J. Crosby and John R. Sweney write:

Tell of the cross where they nailed Him,
Writhing in anguish and pain;
Tell of the grave where they laid Him;
Tell how He liveth again.

Isaac Watts and R.E. Hudson write:

Was it for crimes that I have done
He groaned upon the tree?
Amazing pity, grace unknown,
And love beyond degree!

Charles Wesley and Lewis Edson write:

Five bleeding wounds He bears,
Received on Calvary,
They pour effectual prayers,
They strongly plead for me:
"Forgive him, O forgive," they cry,
"Forgive him, O forgive," they cry,
"Nor let that ransomed sinner die!"

And, "There Is a Green Hill Far Away" by Cecil F. Alexander and George C. Stebbins, "The Old Rugged Cross" by George Bennard, "There is a Fountain" by William Cowper and Lowell Mason, "When I Survey" by Isaac Watts and Lowell Mason, and "He Was Nailed to the Cross For Me" by Frederick A. Graves.

Miller comments, "So rather than railing at the cross with scorn, I must salute the cross, not scorn it. I dare not look at it through eyes of hate; I must exalt it as ultimate love. I never cry that the cross is wretched, but I am. Since that fateful day, I have joined a stream of souls, two thousand years long, each apologizing to the cross for the sinful and unbelieving part of my own nature that produced it."

Your own preachers say this is the basis for our salvation. Again, Miller explains: "We have been saved, not by the Ten Commandments that we could never keep, but by the cross that keeps us and presents us faultless (without sin) and with great joy to our Savior." Consequently, the Cross is significant, according to Schilder, "not as a symbol, but as a bloody reality." In Miller's words, "There is no way to God that does not depend on nails, thorns and wood." After what I've seen and made Jesus endure, "[i]t is sad that we have weaned ourselves from our need of his sacrifice." Why? Because, "[n]o one who believes in Christ and his gospel can get along without the cross."

In case you are wondering, I never scratched or wrote my initials in His cross. The reason? Well, I wasn't really proud of what I had done. But later, I had the feeling He wrote my name in crimson red! In fact, I can truly say, "I was there when they crucified my Lord." And, I fully understand why you sing Philip R. Bliss' song, "Hallelujah! What a Savior!"

14

Thomas

"Then [Jesus] said to Thomas,… 'Stop doubting and believe.'
Thomas said to him, 'My Lord and my God!' "
(John 20:27-28)

I knew Jesus because I doubted His resurrection.

My name is Thomas Didymus, the twin. You know me as "Doubting Thomas."

I suspect most of you have wondered, "What's his problem?" Or, "Why does he have an issue with the Resurrection?"

Well, the answer is, I was dissatisfied with the testimony of my eyes alone. I wanted my hands to have the testimony, as well. My eyes refused to look at what my hands could not touch. In other words, I was not going to believe any heresy about Christ's resurrection.

I was one of Jesus' disciples (Matthew 10:1-4). He chose me because the Father drew me to Him (John 6:44; 17:6, 24). Since then, I tried to be loyal to Jesus and His band of followers. But, I was also full of questions. I wanted to investigate, to inquire so as not to make a blind judgment. In fact, as G. Campbell Morgan writes, "I would not make a confession of faith, of hope, of confidence, unless it was a confession absolutely honest, true to the profoundest convictions of my mind."

Did you know I wasn't the only one who had trouble accepting the Resurrection? Mark reports that the other disciples and Mary Magdalene did not believe it (Mark 16:11). Mary Magdalene assumed Jesus was the gardener (John 20:15). The disciples thought He was a ghost (Luke 24:37). And, the two on the Emmaus road took Him to be a pilgrim visiting the city (Luke 24:18).

Why, then, do people like you label me as the "doubting" one? Richard Exley explains: "Doubt is not a bad thing as much as it is a real thing…. Doubt is an involuntary emotion, while unbelief is an act of the will. Doubt inevitably yields to the power of His presence…. Unbelief…hardens into rebellion. The unbeliever chooses not to believe regardless of the evidence."

Call me "Doubting Thomas," if you like, but I would rather be sincere than political. So, I would not say I believed just to be in Jesus' inner circle. If I did not believe His "creed," I would not recite the "Creed." If I had doubts, I was not going to hide or deny them. To me, being sure was the best way to overcome doubt. After all, Jesus invited Peter: "Look at my hands and my feet. It is I myself! Touch me and see; a ghost does not have flesh and bones, as you see I have" (Luke 24:39).

So, when Jesus insisted He was going to Jerusalem to die, I had a pessimistic outlook on the future. All I could see was loneliness and separation forever. It not only upset my apple-cart, so to speak, it also broke every spoke in its wheels! Oh, the shame of Golgotha!

An old proverb says, "Who soon believes is soon deceived." Solomon agreed, writing, "A fool finds no pleasure in understanding, but delights in airing his own opinions" (Proverbs 18:2). I certainly did not want to be called a "fool." So, I would not even pretend to believe anything of which I was not sure. I mean, I loved Jesus and was happy to have been His follower for three years. But, why did He have to die so young?

My devotion to Jesus included dying for him. I figured we all may die. In fact, I would not have been surprised if we were all arrested in the Garden. I knew my devotion was truly motivated, but I was sad at what might happen if He ventured into Judea. But, quoting Leon Morris, I willingly "chose death with Jesus rather than life without Him."

I do not recommend to anyone what happened next. I had a pity-party for myself. I became a loner and found a corner where I could hang my despair and nurse my doubt.

However, I soon discovered that solitude is not the best medicine for disturbed and saddened hearts. I did not meet regularly with my fellow brothers. My hope was diminished to an empty dream. I saw life through eyes of gloom and despondency. And, as my doubt fermented within me, it fed on itself and began to devour my faith.

Why had I been so demanding? What did I want? Two things. First, I wanted to be equal to my fellow disciples. They followed a certain process before they believed, and I wanted the freedom to follow my process. Second, I needed personal contact. I wanted what we all need, relationships. I wished for a spirit-soul involvement. I required something concrete, something with substance; not abstract or empty fluff. In my heart, I was sincere, and that meant testing all truth by my senses.

The bottom line was, I didn't want a secondhand experience, especially when a firsthand experience was available. Your Apostle Paul had such an experience on the Damascus Road (Acts 9).

When my fellow disciples announced that Jesus was alive, my head said, "Prove it." I would not be cheated by visions and ghosts. My faith was in my hands; flesh must handle flesh. I could not believe in or accept what I could not touch. I was the type of person who must feel the ground under my every step. If you told me to jump across a ditch, I would have to measure it first.

When Jesus was arrested in the Garden, we all ran and left Him with the mob. So, our next meeting was behind closed doors, "for fear of the Jews" (John 20:19). But, I was absent. I was so despondent, I deliberately stayed away. A week later, I was present, and Jesus showed up. As soon as I saw Him, I knew Him, and, from the depths of my soul, I exclaimed, "My Lord and my God!" (John 20:28).

It was most amazing that Jesus came directly to me. He looked me in the eyes and said, "Put your finger here; see my hands. Reach out your hand and put it into my side. Stop doubting and believe" (John 20:27). However, I did not do it. He was alive. All I could say was, "My Lord and my God!"

In spite of all my doubt, Jesus did not rebuke me. Instead, He showed me proofs of His resurrection. He knew I wasn't gullible. So, He honored me with tangible evidence. He showed me His wounds. I immediately recognized Him as my Lord and Savior. He was my Messiah, the Son of God. Like the hymn says,

> *He showed me His hands that were marred for my sinning,*
> *He showed me His feet that were nailed to the tree;*
> *I then saw His brow and His side deeply wounded,*
> *And now I love Jesus, and Jesus loves me.*

During Jesus' ministry, I was aware of three dead people He had raised to life: Lazarus, Jairus' daughter, and the son of the widow from Nain. But, I did not exclaim "My Lord and my God!" to any of them. However, at Jesus' resurrection, I made the declaration, not out of surprise, but because of who Jesus was, and His many predictions that He would rise again.

By the time of Jesus' death, I revered Him as the perfect man. But, after He showed me His wounds, I saw Him as God, my God. In fact, I was the first person to call Him "my God." As Lord, He was the sovereign to whom I submitted. As God, He was deity, whom I would worship. That was the confession on which I based my life. I was still His disciple, and would be forever!

That was my personal confession. I saw Jesus as *my* Lord and *my* God. The risen Jesus belonged to me. From now on, I would serve and acknowledge Him as the only sovereign in my life.

I was present when Jesus promised to take us to many mansions (John 14:1-6). As usual, I questioned Him, saying we didn't know where He was going or how to get there. But, all I needed was Jesus' answer, "I am the way and the truth and the life. No one comes to the Father except through me" (John 14:6).

Before I conclude, I am pleased to tell you I was with the disciples in the Upper Room on the Day of Pentecost (Acts 1:13). We were in prayer, waiting for the power which the Father had promised. On the tenth day, we heard the sound of a violent wind filling the room. We saw flames of fire resting on each of us. Then, as Luke says, "All of them were filled with the Holy Spirit and began to speak in other tongues as the Spirit enabled them" (Acts 2:4).

I want to leave you with an amazing truth: in spite of all my doubts and questions, upon my confession, Jesus did not deny it or denounce me. Rather, He said, "Because you have seen me, you have believed; blessed are those who have not seen and yet have believed" (John 20:29). As Leon Morris says, "belief is belief in one who came from God and who is God."

15

The Penitent Thief

"Then he said, 'Jesus, remember me when you come into your kingdom' "
(Luke 23:42)

I knew Jesus because He took me to Paradise.

My name doesn't matter now. It's a secret between Jesus and me. I like it that way. Besides, Jesus will give me a new name in Paradise. However, most people call me "the penitent thief."

It's not as though I had no name. In fact, in my day, names were more than labels. They meant something. For example, Nabal meant "fool," and Peter, "rock." A person's name was his reputation and character.

Some believed I had a partner in crime and we were connected to Barabbas and his outlaws. I admit, we were murderer-robbers, all condemned to be crucified with Jesus of Nazareth.

Let me allow John Alexander McElroy to describe the scene for you: "There was nothing unusual about an execution as such. Criminals were generally put to death on huge crosses. It was a terrible way to die. Men sometimes hung for days, despite the most awful suffering. And always, at Jerusalem, the executions took place on a hill called Calvary just outside the City. There, everybody could plainly see what happens when you disobey Roman law."

I had disobeyed the law, quickly learning that, in John Calvin Reid's words, "[j]ustice does not balance her books at the close of every day, but in due time they are balanced."

As we hung on our separate crosses, I became connected to Jesus of Nazareth, the mystery man. Abraham Kuyper explains, "The first mystery…is that of Bethlehem's manger. 'God' becomes 'Man.' But a second mystery of even more startling proportions is that of Calvary. The 'Man' becomes a 'Worm' (Psalm 22:6)…. He must be the worm curving Himself in the dust of death."

My robber-friend and I had been criminals together. Now, we were crucified together, paying for our crimes. Sorry at being caught, we were angry with everyone around, especially Jesus. I mean, if He was a miracle worker, why didn't He save us all? So, we joined the crowd in mocking Him (Mark 15:32). However, when I realized He was innocent, my conscience bothered me and I repented (Luke 23:40-41). In fact, I asked Jesus to "remember me" (Luke 23:42) when He inherited His kingdom.

I was surprised I was the only one crying for mercy. And, when I did, I called Jesus by His name, not by His title. Many of your scholars have been shocked that a common thief like me was so free to use Jesus' name.

To this day, people wonder how I got so close to Jesus. Well, it certainly wasn't by going to the synagogue. Nor was it by bowing to an idol, burning incense, singing in the choir, or doing good works. The answer was in the Cross. I put my faith in the Cross. I believed Jesus died for my sin. And, I made it personal by saying, "Jesus, remember me."

That call for mercy was my first and last prayer. Fulton J. Sheen writes: "A dying man asked a dying Man for eternal life; a man without possessions asked a poor man for a kingdom; a thief at the door of death asked to die like a thief and steal Paradise."

It may surprise you that I believed in life after death and "deathbed conversion." Warren W. Wiersbe writes that "this man was not saved at his last opportunity, but at his first opportunity. He was not there when Jesus turned water into wine; he was not there when Jesus stilled the storm or fed the multitude; he did not hear the Sermon on the Mount or Christ's words to the paralytic, 'Your sins are forgiven.' This was his first opportunity to believe on Christ."

The fact is, in His hour of death, Jesus gave me the breath of life. I was a thief, discovering God in a crucifixion. I wish I could have shouted, in Carlyle Marney's words, "Jehovah God! that's my cross he's dying on!"

Now, I wish I could have sung the words of Julia H. Johnston and Daniel B. Towner:

> *Grace, grace, God's grace,*
> *Grace that will pardon and cleanse within;*
> *Grace, grace, God's grace,*
> *Grace that is greater than all my sin.*

Something unusual happened on that hill. With Christ between us, my friend and I were separated in death. And, by my decision to call on Christ, we were separated for eternity. I believed and repented, but he cursed and remained unmoved to the end. As Reid writes: "Dying right beside the Savior of the world, still he stepped out into eternity alone."

One of your poets, Harriet Monroe, puts it like this:

> *To him, the child of darkness, all mercy was denied;*
> *Nailed by his brothers on the cross, he cursed his God and died.*

When Jesus hung in shame on the nails, He was naked and exposed to the world. He suffered physical, mental and emotional humiliation to give me salvation. That was quite a price to satisfy a holy God. Yet, it was a full display of God's love and grace, in Erwin W. Lutzer's words, "given even to those who are at the threshold of death."

Looking at it from Jesus' viewpoint, to be nailed to a cross was shameful enough, but to be hung between two robbers was extreme humiliation. As Lutzer comments, "Jesus was numbered with the transgressors so that you and I could be numbered with the redeemed."

Knowing that, I can relate well to Polycarp, the Bishop of Smyrna, a seaport in Turkey. In 156 A.D., he was burned at the stake for his confession of Christ. Before he died, he was asked to denounce Him. But, he replied, "Eighty and six years have I served Him and He has done me no injustice. How then can I blaspheme my King who has saved me?"

On that account, you may sing for me this hymn by William R. Newell and Daniel B. Towner:

Oh, the love that drew salvation's plan!
Oh, the grace that bro't it down to man!
Oh, the mighty gulf that God did span
At Calvary.

Mercy there was great, and grace was free;
Pardon there was multiplied to me;
There my burdened soul found liberty,
At Calvary.

I concur with John Newton and Edwin O. Excell:

My conscience felt and owned the guilt,
And plunged me in despair,
I saw my sins His blood had spilt,
And helped to nail Him there.

When I felt and admitted my guilt, I was sure of Jesus' pardon. Even as I confessed my faith, my soul soared to the heights of the invisible. Jesus gave me a "blessed assurance" when He answered, "I tell you the truth, today you will be with me in paradise" (Luke 23:43).

Imagine, today! In Paradise!

What did that mean? It meant that "today" and "Paradise" go together. "Today" meant no more waiting. No purgatory. No soul-sleep. No hell. Today, before the sun sets on Golgotha!

"Paradise" meant with Jesus, in the presence of God! "Paradise" meant no more pain and tears! In His nail-pierced hand, Jesus held the key to Paradise. Today, I would take a nonstop flight to be with Him! And, because

He died before me, He was there to welcome me. As Charles H. Spurgeon, your "Prince of Preachers," writes about me, this "man who was our Lord's last companion on earth" was His "first companion at the gates of Paradise." To me, that's all because of the grace of God. As Haldor Lillenas writes:

> *Wonderful grace of Jesus,*
> *Reaching the most defiled,*
> *By its transforming power,*
> *Making him God's dear child,*
> *Purchasing peace and heaven,*
> *For all eternity;*
> *And the wonderful grace of Jesus reaches me.*

Someone has said the ground at the cross is level; that is, we are all the same. God's kingdom is comprised of people who were hopeless. I was among them. Writing about me, Marney says, "This thief could not live a holy life. He could not learn the Lord's prayer or sit at the Lord's table. He could not be a member of a church, he could not be baptized." But today, I would be in Paradise!

As Frederick A. Graves put it:

> *So He gave His life for others*
> *In redeeming this world from sin,*
> *And He's gone to prepare a mansion,*
> *That at last we may enter in.*

When I introduced myself, I said that nobody knew my name. However, Jesus had a name, and it was posted at the top of the Cross. In fact, it was the first gospel tract, proclaiming, "This is the King of the Jews" (Luke 23:38).

Now that I'll be going to Paradise with Jesus, I will receive a name. R. Youngblood writes that, according to "orthodox Judaism a dying person's name is sometimes officially changed in the hope that a new name will bring health and a new life."

Yes, I will have a promotion to a higher status. And, I have Jesus' promise, "I will never blot out his name from the book of life, but will acknowledge his name before my Father and his angels" (Revelation 3:5).

16

Lazarus

"Jesus called in a loud voice, 'Lazarus, come out!'"
(John 11:43)

I knew Jesus because He raised me from the dead.

My name is Lazarus. It's a short form of "Eleazar," an Old Testament word, meaning "God has helped" (Exodus 6:23). And, as you will see, that became quite prophetic.

You know my sisters, Mary and Martha. We lived in Bethany, on the east side of the Mount of Olives, two miles from Jerusalem. As a point of interest, a modern church, bearing my name, has been erected over the ruins of our house in Bethany.

My sisters and I knew Jesus. He called me His friend, in the same way God called Abraham His friend (Isaiah 41:8; James 2:23). In fact, our house was like Jesus' second home. He stayed with us the last week before Passover (Matthew 21:17).

Over time, I became sick, and eventually died. I was dead for four days before Jesus raised me from the dead. Mind you, my death was more than what David A. Redding calls "an expedition into the other world." Nor was my body the only one in what he calls that "community of corpses." But, I was the one resurrected at that time. Interestingly, only the son of the widow of Nain (Luke 7:11-16), Jairus' daughter (Luke 8:41-56), and I could claim such a resurrection. Enoch couldn't, for he did not die (Genesis 5:24). Moses couldn't, for no one knows where God buried him (Deuteronomy 34:5-6). And, Elijah couldn't, for God sent a whirlwind and a chariot of fire to carry him to heaven (1 Kings 2:1-11).

At the time of my sickness, Jesus was in Perea, across the Jordan River, about twenty miles from our home. As you might expect, my sisters notified Jesus. But, what you might not expect is that they waited two days before contacting Him.

As to why they delayed, I learned that, according to Stephen Rexroat, "[t]he only thing more painful than the agony of defeat is the aggravation of delay. Our maturity is tested when we must stand still before we see the salvation of the Lord." The fact is, to quote Trench, "Those whom Christ loves are no more exempt than others from their share of earthly trouble and anguish." Coincidently, my sisters, knowing a storm of malicious envy was circling Jesus' head, did not want to endanger His safety.

When Jesus got the message, He delayed for two days. Why? So He could coincide with the timing of God the Father in bringing Him glory.

Hearing about my sickness, Jesus' immediate response was, "This sickness will not end in death. No, it is for God's glory so that God's Son may be glorified through it" (John 11:4). What did Jesus mean? According to F.F. Bruce, Jesus meant "[t]his illness is not so much one that will terminate in death as one which will demonstrate the glory of God…. The glory of God was to be demonstrated in the raising of Lazarus from death, so that while the illness resulted in temporary death, it resulted more impressively in resurrection and life."

As I understand it, my sickness and death were not the end of the story. Rather, both were for the glory of God. His glory was the end of the story. In fact, the Father and His Son shared a glory that, in Leon Morris' words, "led right on to Calvary."

After two days, Jesus told His disciples He would go to Bethany to resurrect me and comfort my sisters. This would give Him valuable time to help them understand the Resurrection. In other words, according to Homer A. Kent Jr., physical death for me would not be "the final movement of the episode."

Jesus explained that I would rise again. He assured my sisters that resurrection power resided in Him, to give new life. And, He challenged them to believe in Him, because whoever believes in Him "will never die" (John 11:26). As unbelief was the problem then, unbelief is the problem now. In fact, as Kent explains, "The chief cause of unbelief is not inadequate information, but a heart in rebellion against the authority of God and His word."

When Jesus asked my sisters to show Him the tomb, He became overwhelmed and started to quietly cry. His deep grief was not for me only, for He was about to raise me from the dead. But, it was more for the people who failed to understand Him and His mission.

Approaching the tomb, He ordered the stone to the entrance to be moved. According to Jewish law, a grave should not be opened once a stone has been placed against it. As well, it was legally impure to touch a corpse. In fact, people were to stay approximately seven feet from a dead body. Besides, my sister, Martha, warned Jesus that the tomb had a very foul odor. But, Jesus reminded her that the stench was not the end of my story. In fact, He said, if she would but believe, she "would see the glory of God" (John 11:40).

Then, naturally, Jesus looked towards heaven and prayed, "Father, I thank you that you have heard me. I knew that you always hear me, but I said this for the benefit of the people standing here, that they may believe that you sent me." Pausing long enough to catch His breath, He shouted, "Lazarus, come out!" (John 11:41-43).

While I did not see Jesus, I knew that call was for me to take my body and leave death behind. It was as if His voice dispelled the darkness and put my body and soul back together. So, I arose from my cold slab and marched victoriously out the door! If I were a singing man, I would have excelled in the words of Charles Wesley's hymn, "And Can It Be That I Should Gain":

> Long my imprisoned spirit lay,
> Fast bound in sin and nature's night;
> Thine eye diffused a quickening ray—

I woke, the dungeon flamed with light;
My chains fell off, my heart was free,
I rose, went forth, and followed Thee.

When Jesus shouted, "Lazarus, come out!," He was calling me to His side. In that moment, in the blazing noonday sun, I was restored to life in full view of what Fulton J. Sheen calls, "the presence of hostile witnesses." I, once a decaying corpse, walked as if I had never been dead! And that, according to Redding, is "the masterpiece of all the miracles of Christ." That makes it, Kent concludes, "one of the most amazing performances in the career of Jesus."

However, some doubters insist I wasn't actually dead. But, Jesus flatly admitted, "Lazarus is dead" (John 11:14). And, I agreed. After all, I knew I was not soul-sleeping, tossing and turning in unrest. I was not in purgatory, awaiting my sisters to pay my way to heaven. No, I was with Jesus, the Prince of Life, in whose presence no one is ever said to have died. Consequently, He could assure Martha, "I am the resurrection and the life" (John 11:25). That is, the whole power to restore, impart and maintain life resided in Him.

Your Gospel record shows that, when I came from the tomb, my body was still wrapped with cloth. So, Jesus instructed, "Take off the grave clothes and let Him go" (John 11:44). As Augustine noted, "Resurrection must be easier for God than creation out of nothing."

Although I was alive, I was still what George R. Beasley-Murray writes "related to death" and under its power. I would die again. However, when Jesus arose from the dead, He removed His head-cloth because He had, in Beasley-Murray's words, "conquered death definitively himself and will never die again." Death had no more claim on Him. So, He folded His head-cloth separately because God had swallowed up death forever. Like I said, I would eventually die again, but my first resurrection makes me look forward to my second.

As Sheen explains, "If Jesus had said, 'I am the resurrection,' without promising to bestow spiritual and eternal life, there would have been only the promise of reincarnations into successive layers of misery. If He had said, 'I am the life,' without saying, 'I am the resurrection,' we would have merely the promise of our continued discontents. But by combining the two, He affirmed that in Him was a life which, by dying, rises to perfection; therefore death was not the end, but the prelude to a resurrection in the newness and fullness of life. It was a new way of combining the cross and glory."

Personally, I know my resurrection was true. And, one of your early philosophers, Baruch Spinoza, confessed that, "if he could believe the raising of Lazarus, he could tear to shreds his system, and humbly accept the creed of Christians."

Undoubtedly, many of you are asking, "What did your resurrection prove? What did you prove by coming back?"

First, I proved that, sooner or later, we will all pass "through the valley of the shadow of death" (Psalm 23:4). William M. Clow comments, "We live in the midst of struggle and strife...and we continually lament the untimely and desolating death of those we love.... God does not favor and pamper His own with the things of this life. He does not exempt His friends from life's toil and discipline and trial." But, as Kent concludes, "As long as one is fulfilling God's specific plan, and until that plan is accomplished, there is nothing that God's servant need fear."

Second, I proved that all believers need not fear death. Jesus tasted death for all of us, removing its sting. Now, His resurrection guarantees our resurrection. With Charles P. Jones, we can sing:

> *Death has no terrors for the blood-bought one,*
> *O glory hallelujah to the Lamb!*
> *The boasted vict'ry of the grave is gone,*
> *O glory hallelujah to the Lamb!*

Third, I proved that "you can't take it with you."

Fourth, I proved that my tomb was not a cave. It was like a tunnel, with two openings. John Calvin Reid says it's "a passageway through the mountain to the Promised Land. A gate and a stairway to the stars!"

Fifth, I proved that believers should never doubt or worry over their resurrection. Our Master has declared, "[W]hoever lives and believes in me will never die" (John 11:26). And, your Apostle Paul confirms it by saying, "And if the Spirit of him who raised Jesus from the dead is living in you, he who raised Christ from the dead will also give life to your mortal bodies through his Spirit, who lives in you" (Romans 8:11).

Let me assure you that, as a believer in Jesus, I received His love. And, when I died, I saw heaven. But, when He raised me, I returned reluctantly. My four days in heaven were truly "heavenly." Yes, it's a real place, a city.

One of your preachers, R.E. McAlister, describes it like this: "Could you imagine taking a long journey over land and sea, then finally landing on the peaceful shore of eternal deliverance to realize that it's heaven? Could you imagine walking those wonderful streets, and then finding those streets are pure gold like unto transparent glass? Imagine drinking that pure water, and then discovering that that water is from the pure river of the water of life, clear as crystal, proceeding out of the throne of God with the Lamb. Imagine eating that luscious fruit, and then finding that fruit is from the tree of life that beareth twelve manner of fruit and yielded her fruit every month. And the leaves of the tree were for the healing of the nations. Imagine breathing that pure air and then discovering it's celestial. Imagine feeling thrilled from head to foot and then realize that this is immortality. Imagine feeling the touch of a lovely hand and discover it's the nail-pierced hand of the Son of God. Imagine hearing a lovely voice, then realizing that it's the voice of my Savior, the One who led me so tenderly through life and kept me from temptation, and now He presents me before His throne with exceeding joy."

That gives you a glimpse of heaven. That's all I saw, for I was there only four days. But, I can say, "Hallelujah, that's my home! I know because Jesus raised me from the dead!"

As my resurrection showed the end of death, so my new life showed the beginning of glory. However you look at it, my resurrection was a miracle, as was my entry into eternal life. My death was not a miracle, but to raise me was a greater miracle than curing my sickness. Remember, my body was lifeless and my flesh was decaying; so, I needed something more than a splash of cold water on my face. I needed an infusion of Christ's supernatural breath. That's what He gave me. And, that's what displayed Him as the conqueror of death, the giver of life, and the sharer of eternal glory!

17

Cleopas and Mary

"They asked each other, 'Were not our hearts burning within us while he talked with us on the road and opened the Scriptures to us?' "
(Luke 24:32)

We knew Jesus because He opened our eyes to His Word.

Your New Testament calls me Cleopas, which is a short version of Cleopatros (John 19:25). My wife, Mary, and I lived in Emmaus, seven miles northwest of Jerusalem. Most believers say Luke accompanied me on the Emmaus Road, but my wife is the better choice. We were not part of Jesus' twelve disciples, but we were loyal Jews. As His followers, we hoped He would liberate Israel from Roman oppression.

It was Passover time, and we hurried to Jerusalem, to take in the festivities. However, we found few happy campers. The Passover was more low-key than usual. The reason? A mob had crucified Jesus, His grave was empty, and His body was missing. Personally, our faith was shattered and our hope was lost. With our shepherd smitten, the flock soon scattered. So, we headed home.

We were depressed as we slowly trudged to Emmaus. To us, Jerusalem was the accursed city because Jesus had been crucified there. But, worse than that, certain women reported that an angel had told them Jesus was alive, but He was nowhere to be found.

As far as we were concerned, these reports were merely the idle tales of silly women. We didn't even bother checking the empty grave for ourselves. Nor did we wait around Jerusalem until the end of "the third day." We simply wanted to be alone, pamper our disappointment, get home, and forget the whole thing. To us, Israel's redemption was hopeless.

You can imagine how difficult it was to forget. In our sadness, we dragged our feet, asking each other: "Where did you first see Him? Why do you think He was the Christ? What do you remember about His final parable? Do you think we'll ever see Him again? Do you know what I fear? I fear we might have been deceived."

Then, as if out of nowhere, a stranger joined us and walked alongside us. He greeted us pleasantly. But, in our gloom, we failed to recognize Him. Our hearts were too heavy for outside conversation. And, our teary eyes were so blurred we did not know Him. In fact, Mark says: "Afterward Jesus appeared in a different form to two of them while they were walking in the country" (Mark 16:12). So, all three of us continued our silent pace, downward.

The stranger broke the silence. "What are you discussing together as you walk along?," he asked (Luke 24:17).

We stopped dead in our tracks. With a surprised expression on my face, I asked, "Are you only a visitor to Jerusalem and do not know the things that have happened there in these days?" (Luke 24:18). I figured He was a loner in the city. Otherwise, He would have heard of the crucifixion of Jesus of Nazareth. After all, I figured that what was news to me must be news to everybody.

The stranger probed, "What things?" (Luke 24:19).

So, I explained: "About Jesus of Nazareth. He was a prophet, powerful in word and deed before God and all the people. The chief priests and our rulers handed him over to be sentenced to death, and they crucified him; but we had hoped that he was the one who was going to redeem Israel. And what is more, it is the third day since all this took place. In addition, some of our women amazed us. They went to the tomb early this morning but didn't find his body. They came and told us that they had seen a vision of angels, who said he was alive. Then some of our companions went to the tomb and found it just as the women had said, but him they did not see" (Luke 24:19-24).

I mentioned "the third day" because, in the previous three days, everyone in Jerusalem was talking about Jesus' crucifixion. And, besides that, He had promised, "The Son of Man must suffer many things and be rejected by the elders, chief priests and teachers of the law, and he must be killed and on the third day be raised to life" (Luke 9:22). So, Jesus was now in His third day.

As soon as I finished, the stranger replied, "How foolish you are, and how slow of heart to believe all that the prophets have spoken! Did not the Christ have to suffer these things and then enter his glory?" (Luke 24:25-26). In other words, our minds lacked sense, and our affections could not be revived. We were almost like the church at Ephesus, which had left its first love (Revelation 2:4). Our hearts were cold and sluggish, and our passion, lukewarm.

G. Campbell Morgan points out that calling us "foolish" was "His estimate of them, and He knew them. O foolish ones, and slow of heart to believe; and yet He comes to them and joins Himself to them, and walks at their side, and deals with their foolishness, and stirs up the slow heart until it burns and flames."

Then, starting with Moses and all the prophets, the stranger explained, by proper interpretation, how all of Scripture pointed to Himself. That is, in J. Willcock's words, "[i]n studying the Scriptures for Himself He had found Himself in them everywhere."

We were amazed. Who was this mysterious stranger? How did He know all this? Who gave Him such authority? The more He explained the Scriptures, the more we recalled the seed of the woman (Genesis 3:15), the "bronze snake" (Numbers 21:9), the Passover lamb (Exodus 12:1-11), "the scapegoat" (Leviticus 16:8), the "flogging" (Mark 15:15), and the "thirty silver coins" (Matthew 26:15). We remembered the words from the Cross (John 19:26-30), the crown of thorns (John 19:2), the penitent thief (Luke 23:42), and Jesus' final cry, "It is finished" (John 19:30).

That's when our hearts became strangely warm and started to burn with what Willcock calls "the kindling power of a new truth." Our eyes filled with tears. We felt as though we knew Him. In fact, we hoped He could stay with us for the night.

On the outskirts of Emmaus, it appeared like He was going to continue His journey. But, because of His warm presence, and our wish to entertain strangers, we strongly urged Him to be our guest. We said, "Stay with us, for it is nearly evening; the day is almost over" (Luke 24:29). Ordinarily, strangers did not force themselves on anyone, but He accepted our invitation and came to our house.

That night, as was our custom, we gathered at the table to share a meal. Surprisingly, instead of being our guest, He became our host. Sitting between us, He broke and shared the bread.

As we studied His face and hands, it seemed as though we came out of a deep coma, for we suddenly recognized Him! Our discernment related to His revelation, which gave us understanding. Ray Summers writes that, having our eyes "fully opened," we "fully recognized" Him. In Robin R. Meyers' words, the "stranger on the road [was] the risen Lord at the table."

Mysteriously, He was gone. As to why He vanished, we can only conclude that, in David J. Logan's words, we "no longer needed His visual presence." We stared at each other in bewilderment, asking, "Were not our hearts burning within us while he talked with us on the road and opened the Scriptures to us?" (Luke 24:32).

M. Lowrie Hofford and Harrison Millard wrote:

> Abide with me, 'tis eventide!
> Thy walk today with me
> Has made my heart within me burn,
> As I communed with Thee.
> Thy earnest words have filled my soul
> And kept me near Thy side.

Isn't it interesting that our hearts did not burn while we talked with each other and with Him? They burned only when He talked with us. Summers explains: "The warm glow came in what he said as he opened the Scriptures." When we stopped talking and listened to Him, our hearts became ablaze. Obviously, listening to and understanding the Scriptures is a real "eye-opener."

In his poem, "Conversation," your own poet, William Cowper, puts it like this:

> *The humble Stranger soon became their guest,*
> *And, made so welcome at their simple feast,*
> *He blessed the bread, but vanished at the word,*
> *And left them both exclaiming, "Twas the Lord!*
> *Did not our hearts feel all He deigned to say?*
> *Did not they burn within us by the way?"*

That was enough. We were convinced. So, we sprang to our feet and headed back to Jerusalem, to share our newfound joy and renewed hope. There, we found the Eleven, who announced, "It is true! The Lord has risen and has appeared to Simon" (Luke 24:34). We then told what happened to us on the road, and how we recognized Him when He broke and shared the barley-bread. True, the Cross was behind us, but it took only a little piece of bread to stir the remembrance of our roots.

Fortunately, the risen Jesus restored our faith and gave us new hope. We related again. We were family. We relied on Him and supported each other. His resurrection became the glory of our Christian faith, and His table, the center for fellowship.

Fanny J. Crosby and William H. Doane express it well:

> *Near the cross! O Lamb of God,*
> *Bring its scenes before me;*
> *Help me walk from day to day,*
> *With its shadows o'er me.*

Looking back, we were embarrassed that we did not recognize Jesus. As He lamented, we were slow to believe and refused to be spiritually alert. Perhaps some of you have embarrassed yourselves in the same way. For example, how often does Jesus come to you and you do not discern

Him? Whatever your case, Alexander MacLaren assures us that "Jesus is not repelled by doubts and perplexities, if they are freely spoken to Him." In fact, knowing us is the key to our relationship. As Meyers points out, Jesus will "not leave us alone even when we are hurt and disappointed, even when it seems that the best and the brightest in life is destroyed. The death of Jesus could no more stop the love of God than the night could turn back the morning."

Our loss of faith and hope resulted in deep depression. As W.H. Burnett contends, when we make Jesus "a distant unrecognized figure" in our lives, we get "a diminished view of Christ and His Person [and] a distorted view of divine purpose and control."

It was somewhat amusing that we reported to Jesus about Jesus, without even knowing Him. But, according to Burnett, we came full circle—from "broken hearts to burning hearts, from closed minds to opened understanding and from heavens that seemed like brass, to opened heavens that received our Lord into glory!"

18

Paul

"I thank Christ Jesus our Lord, who has given me strength, that
he considered me faithful, appointing me to his service"
(1 Timothy 1:12)

I knew Jesus because He "arrested" me on the Damascus Road.
I had two names and I lived two lives. First, I was Saul, an enemy of
Christ. Second, I became Paul, a missionary for Christ.

I was born in the Gentile city of Tarsus in Cilicia, and reared by
devout Jewish parents (Philippians 3:5). In Jerusalem, I studied at the feet
of Gamaliel, the most famous Jewish rabbi (Acts 5:34). I believed in God
and was zealous to do something for Him.

For as long as I can remember, I had heard of Christ and encountered
many of His followers, "Christians," as they called themselves. They said
Jesus had been crucified, but had risen from the dead. To me, that didn't
make sense. They called Him Messiah, but to me, that was blasphemy. I
wasn't going to believe such superstition. In fact, I would start a campaign
to stop it and destroy the followers, if necessary. After all, wouldn't that be
my "service to God" (John 16:2)?

Our first mission was to stone Stephen. I even held the coats of the
murderers while they pelted him to death (Acts 7:43-60).

I then organized such a persecution against the Christian church in Jerusalem that the Christians scattered everywhere. I obtained letters from the Sanhedrin, the Jewish council (Acts 26:11-12), to capture Christians in Damascus, 140 miles northeast of Jerusalem. As the capital of Syria and the center for commercial trade routes, Christianity was flourishing and beginning to spread around the world.

It would take my companions and me five to seven days to walk to Damascus. Once there, I would arrest those belonging to the Jesus "Way," bring them in chains to Jerusalem, and imprison them (Acts 9:1-2).

However, before I reached Damascus, Jesus "arrested" me. At noon, the same Jesus I had despised, and whose followers I had attacked, struck me to the ground by the brightness of His glory. But, it was not out of vengeance; He did not mean to destroy me. It was out of love and to call me into His service.

Behind the light, which blinded my eyes, I heard Him ask, "Saul, Saul, why do you persecute me?" (Acts 9:4). Obviously, He knew me before I knew Him. Surprised, I replied, "Who are you, Lord?" (Acts 9:5). Really, I was saying, "You are the Lord, aren't you?" And, He answered, "I am Jesus whom you are persecuting" (Acts 9:5). I was convinced and, in the words of John Calvin Reid, "realized that He who could thus read my conscience had the right to rule it." So, I surrendered by asking what He wanted me to do.

William Barclay writes that I "intended to enter Damascus like an avenging fury, [but] was led by the hand into that city, blind and helpless as a child."

In my persecution tactics, I was like a stubborn ox, kicking the spikes at the front of the cart (Acts 9:5). I protested becoming a servant of Christ. I was haunted by Gamaliel's warning (Acts 5:33-39), Stephen's sermon (Acts 7), and the dedication of Christians. My conscience was so "pricked" by this, I began to think Jesus might be the Messiah, after all.

When Christ confronted me on the Damascus Road, I had a dramatic conversion, especially since God initiated it. He sought and found me, and I did not resist. There, He changed my name to Paul, and told me to go into Damascus and wait for further instructions (Acts 9:6). As a result of the dazzling light, I was blind for three days. I felt alone until Ananias, a disciple, befriended me. As Reid writes, "Through his prayers my sight was restored and by his hand I was baptized."

When I related my conversion story in some of the synagogues, the Jews were furious in unbelief. They would have killed me had not my friends lowered me in a basket over the wall at night (Acts 9:25). From there, I went into the deserts of Arabia for three years (Galatians 1:17), praying and meditating on the significance of Christ's birth, death and resurrection.

I returned to Jerusalem, where the Apostles kept me "at arm's length," almost as an untouchable. They did not believe my conversion experience. However, according to Reid, Barnabas "believed in my sincerity and persuaded the Apostles to accept me."

One of my worst frustrations was my "thorn in the flesh" (2 Corinthians 12:1-10). I prayed three times for the Lord to remove it, but, instead, He gave me grace to endure it. Through that experience, I learned that, as Reid writes, "[i]f you lack that measure of grace, perhaps the reason is that in your praying you are too intent upon the thing you are praying for, and not intent enough upon the God to whom you pray."

To begin my missionary service, through Ananias, the Lord said, "This man is my chosen instrument to carry my name before the Gentiles and their kings and before the people of Israel. I will show him how much he must suffer for my name" (Acts 9:15-16). That's when I was "appointed a herald and an Apostle and a teacher" (2 Timothy 1:11). In fact, He has "given me strength. That He considered me faithful, appointing me to this service. Even though I was once a blasphemer and a persecutor and a violent man, I was shown mercy because I acted in ignorance and unbelief" (1 Timothy 1:12-13).

What did I believe and teach? I preached about my "revelation of Jesus Christ" (Galatians 1:11-12) on the Damascus Road. Freely I had received, freely I would give. So, I traveled extensively, talking to people about Christ, simply passing on the tradition I received, emphasizing Jesus, the Son of God (1 Corinthians 15:3-8).

As part of my call into the ministry, I made four missionary journeys.

My first journey is recorded in Acts 13:1-14:28. The church in Antioch sent Barnabas and me to Salamis, with John Mark as our assistant. After preaching in Salamis, we traveled to Paphos, then by boat to Perga, where Mark left us. We then ministered in Antioch in Pisidia, Iconium, Derbe and Lystra, where I was stoned and left for dead (Acts 14:6-20). On that mission, we instructed converts and organized them into churches. From Attalia, we sailed back to Antioch in Syria.

My second journey is recorded in Acts 15:36-18:22. Because of a conflict with Barnabas, for that trip I chose Silas to accompany me. We left Antioch in Syria and traveled to Derbe and Lystra, visiting churches in Syria. Timothy joined us at Lystra, and the three of us traveled through Phrygia and Galatia. At Troas, some people in Macedonia called for us to come and help them (Acts 16:8-9). There, we founded churches at Philippi, Thessalonica and Berea. Upon reaching Athens, on Mar's Hill I preached about "The Unknown God" (Acts 17:18-34). Leaving Athens, we started a church at Corinth, and, from there, sailed to Ephesus and Caesarea, and visited Jerusalem.

My third journey is recorded in Acts 18:23-21:16. From Antioch in Syria, I caught a ship to Ephesus and, along the way, encouraged the churches in Galatia and Phrygia. I spent twenty-seven months teaching and preaching in Ephesus. Eventually, my preaching provoked the silversmiths, and Demetrius led a riot that ended my ministry there (Acts 19:13-41). After three months in Greece, I sailed from Philippi to Troas, then to Miletus, where I boarded a ship for Tyre, and continued on to Jerusalem.

My fourth journey is recorded in Acts 21:17-28:31. I was arrested in Jerusalem and, under heavy guard, was sent to Caesarea, where I was jailed for two years. Felix, Festus and Agrippa heard my case, but when I appealed to Caesar, I was shipped off to Rome, accompanied by Luke and Aristarchus. At Myra, we transferred to a grain boat headed for Italy. For fourteen days, we survived a typhoon, but the boat was wrecked on the island of Malta. Three months later, we continued to Rome, where I was placed in custody.

No pun intended, but a lot of water has flowed under the bridges of my life, all in the pursuit of my calling. When I was Saul of Tarsus,

I was the church's public enemy number one. But when I met Christ, God performed the greatest reversal in all history. He changed me from Christ's enemy to Christ's ambassador to the Gentiles. After thirty years of ministry, I had fought a good fight, finished the race, and kept the faith (2 Timothy 4:7). And, after Nero executed me in 66 A.D., I departed to receive the crown of righteousness from the Lord Himself.

By learning of Jesus, I got to learn more about myself. So, I confessed to the Romans, "I am unspiritual, sold as a slave to sin...nothing good lives in me, that is, in my sinful nature" (Romans 7:14, 18). However, I assured them I was not ashamed of the gospel of Christ (Romans 1:16), and "that in all things God works for the good of those who love him, who have been called according to his purpose" (Romans 8:28).

By following Jesus, I was able to tell the Corinthians, "For I resolved to know nothing while I was with you except Jesus Christ and Him crucified" (1 Corinthians 2:2).

By learning about Jesus, I taught the Galatians that "a man is not justified by observing the law, but by faith in Jesus Christ" (Galatians 2:16).

By understanding Jesus, I urged the Ephesians to know the love of Christ "that surpasses knowledge" (Ephesians 3:19).

By believing in Jesus, I encouraged the Philippians regarding "the power of his resurrection and the fellowship of sharing in his sufferings, becoming like him in his death, and so, somehow, to attain to the resurrection from the death" (Philippians 3:10).

Ever since my dramatic conversion and commission on the Damascus Road, I wanted to learn more about Christ. I wanted to experience Him through faith. First, as my Redeemer. Then, He would renew my life by His resurrection, whereby the Spirit, who raised Him from physical death, would raise me from spiritual death. Eventually, that same Spirit would raise me from literal death (Romans 8:11).

However, such a relationship would be costly. I would have to bear my cross, or crucify my flesh (Galatians 2:20), in order to identify with Him in His sufferings (Colossians 1:24). I found that, to share His life was to share His sufferings, and I was honored to do so (2 Corinthians 1:24).

By knowing Jesus through faith, I reminded the Colossians that since their life was hidden in Christ, "[w]hen Christ, who is your life, appears, then you will also appear with him in glory" (Colossians 3:4).

By trusting Jesus, I comforted the Thessalonians not "to grieve like the rest of men who have no hope, [because] God will bring with Jesus those who have fallen asleep in him [and] we will not precede them [for] the dead in Christ will rise first [then] we will be caught up together with them in the clouds to meet the Lord in the air. And so we will be with the Lord forever" (1 Thessalonians 4:13-18).

By hoping in Jesus, I declared to Timothy that "I am not ashamed, because I know whom I have believed, and am convinced that he is able to guard what I have entrusted to him for that day" (2 Timothy 1:12).

Appendix

Poems by Clarence Dawe, the author's father

Wist Ye Not?

"Wist ye not?" said Jesus,
"My Father's work I do.
"Wist ye not?" said Jesus,
"It is all for you."

"Wist ye not?" said Jesus,
"I'm He who says to thee:
A well of living water
Is springing up from Me."

"Wist ye not?" said Jesus,
"He who will believe,
Pardon and redemption
This moment shall receive."

"Wist ye not?" said Jesus,
"These wondrous works I do.
My promise I have given
That you may do them, too."

"Wist ye not?" said Jesus,
"My name in heaven is great.
All things I have promised
To those who ask in faith."

"Wist ye not?" said Jesus,
"This mountain standing by,
For just one grain of faith
In yonder sea shall lie."

"Wist ye not?" said Jesus,
"Do you believe all this?
My promise is sure and steadfast
But do not ask amiss."

The Backslider

Once you loved the Savior
And trusted in His Word;
Now you are so wayward
As though you never heard
The story of salvation,
His mercy full and free;
With Christ's own salutation
"My suffering was for thee."

Tonight you are so lonely.
Tonight you are so cold.
You know the Savior loves you,
But you've wandered from His fold.

You have wandered from the Savior
In the barren fields afar.
But the Savior still is whispering:
"The door is but ajar."

There are loved ones waiting for you,
Mothers and sisters, too;
And children praying for you,
Won't you start your life anew?

This Man

We read in the Bible
God's wonderful plan,
Hidden through the ages,
Yet revealed in this Man.

This Man, in the beginning,
All things He has made,
Our life and our health,
Our sunshine and shade.

God brought forth His Word
In the flesh for awhile,
To show by example
And set free from exile.

When on the Cross
It was all He could do;
He cried, "It is finished,
I have pardon for you."

His Father in heaven
Heard the cries of His Son;
Though forgotten for a moment,
Was the work of grace begun.

Now He lives triumphant
Over death and sin,
To justify forever
Those who enter in.

Yesterday He created,
Today He makes anew.
Tomorrow He'll seal forever
The work He came to do.

This World

The world is very silent
To those who cannot hear.
The world is full of noises
To those filled with fear.

The world doesn't move at all,
To those who cannot see.
But to those who see it most,
The world becomes a moving host.

The world is void and empty
To those who cannot touch.
But to those with so many things
The world is oh, so much.

The world goes by so odorless
To those who cannot smell.
But the fragrance of His presence
They surely love to tell.

It is He who gives the hearing,
The smell and also sight.
But, oh to touch His garments
Makes everything come right.

We speak about the Savior
Who walked Judea's sod;
To give His life and power
To man from Father God.

Today, if you will hear Him,
And trust His Word and grace
He'll meet whatever problem
In life you have to face.

Last Night's Meditation

Last night in meditation late,
My soul entered heaven's gate;
And there upon the streets of gold,
The Blessed One had full control.

He showed to me those mansions fair,
With harps to play and crowns to wear;
And countless saints in spotless white,
Beholding Him who is the Light.

Last night in meditation long,
My soul was filled with bursts of song;
How wondrous was that place to me,
To sit, Dear Lord, and sing of Thee.

Last night in meditation sweet,
I sat alone at Jesus' feet.
As holy stillness settled there,
I knew my Lord had answered prayer.

Last night in meditation deep,
I felt the Holy Spirit sweep;
Who took me to new heights above,
To overwhelm me with His love.

When all the host began to sing
Loud Hallelujahs to the King,
I joined in triumph to proclaim
That I was there in Jesus' Name.

My Hope

As you look on me, you will see,
This is all that's left of me.
My soul has gone to be with God,
This will go beneath the sod.

But when the trump shall sound again,
Reechoing over every plain,
This part of me shall then arise
To join the other in the skies!

Made anew this body puts on
The immortality of the Son.
To live before eternal eyes,
For Christ has opened Paradise.

Then when before the Judgment Seat
This body and soul will be complete.
I'll answer when my name is given,
And enter all the joys of heaven.

To the Marriage Supper I will go,
All dressed in raiment white as snow;
To gather where the feast is spread,
And see our Great Exalted Head.
The Servant will be Christ the Son
For He is God the Three-in-one.

And when He shall return, the King,
The New Jerusalem He will bring.
With high wall and twelve foundations
Unto her shall gather nations.

The Lord, so good and true,
Says once again, "I make things new."
And we shall dwell in glory bright
Where never come end or night.

NOTE: At Dad's request, this poem was read at his funeral and a copy placed on his casket (December 14, 1988).

My Vision of Jesus

I have a vision of Jesus
Each day as I read His Word.
I see Him with His Beloved,
They call her "The Great Speckled Bird."

I see Him every morning
As all the days are born;
He sets His clock in motion–
The moon, the stars, the sun.

I see Him every evening
When time shall be no more;
The sun refuses its shining,
And the moon in bloody gore.

I see Him on the mountains
Commanding a great stone;
To dash in pieces all kingdoms
When He comes to set up His own.

I see Him in Jerusalem,
The King in Royal state;
The cry goes up, "Hosanna,
Lift high the Eastern Gate!"

Works Cited

Barclay, William. *The Acts of the Apostles*. The Daily Study Bible. Edinburgh: Saint Andrews, 1953.

———. *James and Peter*. Toronto, ON: G.R. Welch, 1976.

———. *The Letters to Philippians, Colossians and Thessalonians*. Toronto, ON: G.R. Welch, 1975.

Baxter, J. Sidlow. *Awake, my Heart: Daily Devotional Studies for the Year*. Grand Rapids, MI: Zondervan, 1960.

Beasley-Murray, George R. *John*. Word Biblical Commentary, vol. 36. Waco, TX: Word, 1987.

Binns, Walter Pope. *Behold the Man!* Nashville, TN: Broadman, 1960.

Bishop, J. Bashford, *Pentecostal Evangel*, August 28, 1977.

Bruce, F.F. *The Epistle to the Hebrews*. Grand Rapids, MI: Eerdmans, 1979.

———. *The Gospel of John*. Grand Rapids, MI: Eerdmans, 1983.

Burnett, W.H., "The Emmaus Road," *Counsel*, March-April 1992.

Chappell, Clovis G. *Faces About the Cross*. Grand Rapids, MI: Baker, 1976

Clarke's Commentary, Adam. http://e-sword.net

Clow, William M. *The Idylls of Bethany*. London: Hodder & Stoughton, 1969.

Communicator. April 2009. Nazarene Publishing House.

Cowman, L.B. Ed., James Reimann. *Streams in the Desert*. Grand Rapids, MI: Zondervan, 1996 [1925].

Denny, Randal Earl. *In the Shadow of the Cross: Walk With Jesus From the Garden to the Tomb*. Eugene, OR: Wipf & Stock, 2007.

Edersheim, Alfred. *The Life and Times of Jesus the Messiah*, vol. 2. Peabody, MA: Hendrickson, n.d.

"Eve's Lamentation (From the Early Irish)" http://books.google.com/books?id'VGZfvHtY2AsC&pg'PA33&dq 'since+of+heaven+I+robbed+my+race&cd'2#v'onepage&q'since%20 of%20heaven%20I%20robbed%20my%20race&f'false

Exley, Richard, *Pentecostal Evangel*. April 12, 1998.

Fenelon, Francois, http://www.worldofquotes.com/author/ Fran!ccedil;ois-F!eacute;nelon/1/index.html.

Foucauld, Charles de, quoted in *In Touch* magazine 2/01.

Fruchtenbaum, Arnold. *Table Talk*.

Gill, John, quoted in http://www.e-sword.net/features.html

Gooding, David. *According to Luke*. Grand Rapids, MI: Eerdmans, 1987.

Griffith, Leonard. *Gospel Characters: The Personalities Around Jesus*. Grand Rapids, MI: Eerdmans, 1976.

Hankins, Barry. *Francis Schaeffer and the Shaping of Evangelical America*. Grand Rapids, MI: Eerdmans, 2008.

Hastings, James, ed. *The Great Texts of the Bible: St. John*. New York: Charles Scribner's Sons, 1912.

Hodge, Charles. *Romans*. Wheaton, IL: Crossway, 1993.

Jamieson, Robert; A.R. Fausett; David Brown. *A Commentary, Critical and Explanatory, on the Old and New Testaments*, vol. II. New York: S.S. Scranton, 1875.

Johnson, James Weldon, *50 Plus*, April 2006.

Josephus, Flavius. *Antiquities of the Jews*.

Kent, Homer A., Jr. *Light in the Darkness: Studies in the Gospel of John*. Winona Lake, IN: BMH Books, 2005.

——, "Matthew," in Everett F. Harrison, ed. *The Wycliffe Bible Commentary*. New Testament. Chicago, IL: Moody, 1962.

Krummacher, Frederick W. *The Suffering Savior*. Chicago, IL: Moody, n.d.

Kuyper, Abraham. *His Decease at Jerusalem*. Grand Rapids, MI: Eerdmans, 1946.

Loane, Marcus L. *John the Baptist as Witness and Martyr*. Grand Rapids, MI: Zondervan, 1968.

____. *The Place Called Calvary*. Grand Rapids, MI: Zondervan, 1968.

Lockyer, Henry. *In Touch*.

Logan, David J. *Choice Gleanings*, n.d.

Lutzer, Erwin W. *Cries from the Cross: A Journey into the Heart of Jesus*. Chicago, IL: Moody, 2002.

MacArthur, John. *The MacArthur Study Bible*. Nashville, TN: Nelson, 2006.

MacLaren, Alexander. *The Gospel According to St. Luke*. London: Hodder & Stoughton, 1908.

____. *St. John (Chapters 15-21)*. London: Hodder & Stoughton, 1907.

Marney, Carlyle. *He Became Luke Us: The Words of Identification*. New York: Abingdon, 1964.

Marsh, F.E. *The Structural Principles of the Bible*. Grand Rapids, MI: Kregel, 1969.

____. *Why Did Christ Die?* Grand Rapids, MI: Zondervan, n.d.

McAlister, R.E., "Jerusalem the Golden," in *Heaven's Strategy and Other Sermons*. Toronto, ON: privately published, n.d.

McElroy, John Alexander. *Living with the Seven Words*. Nashville, TN: Abingdon, 1961.

McWhirter, G. Stuart. *The Evangelist's Perspective*. Spring 2003.

Meyers, Robin R., in *Biblical Preaching Journal*, Spring 1990.

Miller, Calvin. *Once Upon a Tree: Devotional Essays on the Cross*. West Monroe, LA: Howard, 2002.

Morgan, G. Campbell. *The Westminster Pulpit*, vols. I-II. Fincastle, VA: Scripture Truth Book, n.d.

Morris, Leon. *Jesus is the Christ*. Grand Rapids, MI: Eerdmans, 1989.

_____. *John*. Grand Rapids, MI: Eerdmans, 1971.

Papini, Giovanni. *Life of Christ*. New York: Harcourt, Brace & Co., 1923.

Pfeiffer, Charles F., and Everett F. Harrison, eds. *The Wycliffe Bible Commentary: A Phrase by Phrase Commentary of the Bible*. Chicago, IL: Moody, 1962.

Redding, David A. *The Miracles of Christ*. Westwood, NJ: Revell, 1964.

Reid, John Calvin. *We Knew Jesus: A Series of Lenten Messages*. Grand Rapids, MI: Eerdmans, 1954.

Rexroat, Stephen, in *Pentecostal Evangel*, June 23, 1991.

Rhodes, Ron. *What Did Jesus Mean? Making Sense of the Difficult Sayings of Jesus*. Eugene, OR: Harvest House, 1999.

Rimmer, Harry. *The Crucible of Calvary*. Grand Rapids, MI: Eerdmans, 1940.

Robertson's Word Pictures, http://e-sword.net

Sangster, W.E. *They Met at Calvary: Were You There?* London: Epworth, 1956.

Scarborough, Lynn Wilford. *Talk Like Jesus.* Beverly Hills, CA: Phoenix, 2007.

Schilder, Klass. *Christ Crucified.* Grand Rapids, MI: Eerdmans, 1940.

____. *Christ in His Suffering.* Grand Rapids, MI: Eerdmans, 1938.

____. *Christ on Trial.* Grand Rapids, MI: Eerdmans, 1939.

Shakespeare, William. *Julius Caesar.*

Sheen, Fulton J. *Life of Christ.* New York: McGraw-Hill, 1958.

Stalker, James M. *The Trial and Death of Jesus Christ.* Grand Rapids, MI: Zondervan, 1961.

Stevenson, Herbert F. *The Road to the Cross.* Westwood, NJ: Fleming H. Revell, 1962.

Stevenson, J.G. *The Judges of Jesus.* London: James Clarke & Co., 1909.

Stott, John, http://gospeldelta.com/2010/01/john-stott-on-suffering-if-it-were-not-for-the-cross/

Summers, Ray. *Commentary on Luke.* Waco, TX: Word, 1972.

Tenney, Merrill C. *In Touch.*

Tholuck, Friedrich August. *Light From the Cross: Sermons on the Passion of Our Lord*. Trans. R.C. Lundon Brown. Chicago, IL: Moody Press, 1952 [1869].

Todd, Galbraith Hall. *Culture and the Cross*. Grand Rapids, MI: Baker, 1959.

Whyte, Alexander. *Bible Characters*. Edinburgh: Oliphants Ltd., n.d.

Willcock, J. T*he Preacher's Complete Homiletic Commentary on the Gospel According to St. Luke*. London: Funk & Wagnalls, 1896.

Youngblood, R. "Names in Bible Times, Significance of," in Walter A. Elwell, ed., *Evangelical Dictionary of Theology*. Grand Rapids, MI: Baker Book House, 1984.

Acknowledgements

I want to express my gratitude to the various authors and publishers, whose works I used. I have endeavored to find authors and/or publishers to give due credit for my sources. Unfortunately, some are unknown. However, if any have been overlooked, I apologize and will give proper recognition in a future edition.

I am deeply indebted to my longtime friend, my editor, Burton K. Janes, for his tireless work with my first manuscript. A prolific author in his own right, he writes with variety–color, emotion and knowledge. After reading Burton, you've had an experience. Thanks, my friend.

I am truly grateful to Pastor Roy D. King, my behind-the-scenes mentor for almost fifty years. He has served my denomination, the Pentecostal Assemblies of Newfoundland and Labrador, in different capacities and with distinction, concluding as General Superintendent for sixteen years. My fellow pastors know him as "RD," and respect him affectionately. As a preacher, he speaks with clarity and conviction and, as a writer, he has a creative pen. Thanks, "RD."

In the initial stages of my book, I was fortunate to have many friends who reviewed various chapters: Redena Paddock, Ronald Dawe, Lillian Whitt, Karen Janes-Winsor, Bishop Donald Young, Pastor Roy D. King, Rev. Elliott Baker, Rev. Tina Strutt, Donald Hennessey, Maureen Dawe, Valmond Head, Flora Boyd and Doreen Dawe.

Special appreciation and love go to my wife, Laura, and our four children, Barbara Freake, Michael, Tina Strutt and Richard. I am proud of you all.

ABOUT THE AUTHOR

George Henry Dawe is a retired pastor with the Pentecostal Assemblies of Newfoundland and Labrador. Graduating from Eastern Pentecostal Bible College (EPBC), Peterborough, Ontario, in 1962, he taught school, lectured at EPBC, pastored six churches, and founded Family Enrichment Ministries. He has three earned Master's degrees and is listed in *Who's Who Among Students in American Universities & Colleges 1978-1979*. He and his wife, Laura, of fifty years, reside in Norris Arm North, Newfoundland and Labrador, and have four children and thirteen grandchildren. George enjoys reading, writing, preaching and laughing.